Wirral Walks

Anthony Annakin-Smith

2nd Edition © Anthony Annakin-Smith, 2010

1st edition published 2005, reprinted 2007

Published by Sigma Leisure – an imprint of
Sigma Press, Stobart House, Pontyclerc, Penybanc Road
Ammanford, Carmarthenshire SA18 3HP

British Library Cataloguing in Publication Data

A CIP record for this book is available from the British Library

ISBN: 978-1-85058-851-1

Typesetting and Design by: Sigma Press, Ammanford, Carms

Maps: © Bute Cartographics

Photographs: © Anthony Annakin-Smith (unless otherwise stated)

Cover photograph: Thurstaston

Printed by: Cromwell Press Group, Trowbridge, Wiltshire

Every effort has been made to fulfil requirements with regard to reproducing copyright material. The author and publisher will be glad to rectify any ommisions at the earliest opportunity.

Disclaimer: The information in this book is given in good faith and is believed to be correct at the time of publication. Care should always be taken when walking in hill country. Where appropriate, attention has been drawn to matters of safety. The author and publisher cannot take responsibility for any accidents or injury incurred whilst following these walks. Only you can judge your own fitness, competence and experience. Do not rely solely on sketch maps for navigation: we strongly recommend the use of appropriate Ordnance Survey (or equivalent) maps.

Foreword by Mike McCartney:
Cultural Ambassador for Wirral

Those of us who live on the Wirral realise how fortunate we are in having such an interesting and varied landscape so close to home. If we want to explore open spaces we can choose the contrasts of farming country or beach; marshland or heath; woods or parkland. Walking doesn't only help us see the Wirral – it's also a great way to shed those extra pounds and look after our hearts. And if we want to delve into Wirral's rich cultural history we can find places with links to prehistoric man, through thousands of years of history including the Vikings, up to the development of industrial England. It is a privilege to be Cultural Ambassador for an area of such diversity.

Furthermore, what makes Wirral particularly special is that all this heritage and culture is so easily accessible, in fact right on our doorsteps! We have an excellent network of footpaths and other walker-friendly routes just waiting to be explored. But that's for us Wirralians ... we're OK, but are you one of the lucky ones?

And where to walk?

As luck would have it, all our problems are solved with Anthony Annakin-Smith's book of 'Wirral Walks'. Not only does it suggest some great walking routes but it also explains what we can see along the way, bringing Wirral's scenic and historic heritage to life.

I am sure you will enjoy using this book and wish you many happy hours exploring the rich landscape that Wirral has to offer. If I bump into you en route, don't forget to say 'Hi'!

Yours walkingly

Mike McCartney

Preface to Second Edition

I'm delighted that there is to be a second edition to this book. It shows how much interest there is in walking generally, and walking the Wirral's beautiful countryside in particular.

This edition contains two new walks – both fantastic routes in my view (admittedly biased!). There are also major revisions to several other routes. l am constantly amazed at how much the landscape changes in a short period of time – changes that affect the directions in the walks. These changes can vary from simple things like the removal of a fence or bench to massive engineering works such as the changes to the A550 which transformed (for the worse!) the route to wonderful Shotwick Castle. Every walk direction has been checked for this new edition (and the Shotwick Castle route radically changed to make it even more of a stunner!).

Once again I need to thank many people for helping me in various ways to bring out this new edition. In addition to the names below I should mention Sue Craggs, Hilary Morris and Rob Gregory. And definitely not forgetting my wife Ruth, in our 25th wedding anniversary year, who re-trod the walks with me.

I hope you will enjoy this new edition of 'Wirral Walks'.

Anthony Annakin-Smith

If you have any comments or queries about Wirral Walks, or if you become aware of changes to the route directions, please do write to me at: **wirralwalks@hotmail.com**

Some time in the near future I hope to set up a Wirral Walks website (wirralwalks.org.uk), Facebook account and maybe join Twitter. These will be great ways for all 'Wirral Walkers' to keep in touch, posting new information and sharing it with each other. The sites aren't set up yet but do check 'Wirral Walks' from time to time to see if I've caught up with the technology!

Preface to the First Edition

I hope this book will appeal to two kinds of people.

First, if you're someone who just wants a refreshing local walk but doesn't know where to go, it suggests routes to follow – 27 in fact. These range from those that are suitable for parents with young children to full-day ones for more adventurous walkers.

Second, if you're the type of person who's curious about what you see along the way, it aims to answer the kind of questions you might ask. Why are there so many ponds on the Wirral? What made them put that lighthouse there? When was that rock carving made? Why are there so many village names ending in 'by'? Who decided to put a fifth clock on that church tower? And so on. In this respect, I hope that armchair readers can get as much from the book as walkers.

For me, walks prompt a never-ending series of questions. I hope this book will answer at least some of yours.

Acknowledgements

If you like this book it's probably because so many people helped me to write it – in lots of different ways. These include:

Rodney Wright and Jen Lewis for their inspirational teaching and leadership on the Diploma in Landscape Interpretation at the University of Liverpool. Hazel Clark, Jo Crossley and the Department of History team at Chester College also deserve a mention.

The countryside rangers at Leasowe, Hilbre, Thurstaston, Royden Park, Eastham, Rivacre, Dibbinsdale and Hadlow Station, employed by either Wirral Borough Council or Cheshire County Council. They were invariably very helpful and full of good information.

Dennis Tomlinson, the author of *West Kirby and Beyond – An RAF National Serviceman looks back* (Ameliel Press), price £8.50, for kindly allowing me to reproduce the photo on page 64.

Many other people helped in different ways. In particular I should mention Paul Loughnane, Rusty Keane, Gavin Hunter, Mike McCartney and Chris Holbrook. Also, those who allowed me to use their photos – names are given alongside the photos, where appropriate.

Thank you also to the many people of Wirral who contributed but whose names I never knew. Not one person ever objected to being in a camera shot, offering information or (occasionally) letting me onto their private land.

Finally thanks to Ruth for proofreading and to Ruth and my children James and Claire for 'road-testing' the walks and for allowing me the time to write all this!

Anthony Annakin-Smith

Contents

Introduction

Many of these walking routes first appeared in a local magazine, Wirral Essence. Over the four years they were published, I was encouraged to receive many comments from people who had enjoyed them – both walkers and 'armchair ramblers' who enjoyed reading the routes as much as treading them. Several people suggested compiling the routes into a book and 'Wirral Walks', now in its second edition, was the result.

The book gave me an opportunity to add several routes to those that appeared in the magazine. It also gave me the space to say much more about the beautiful and fascinating local landscape. For me, one of the many pleasures of walking – besides the fresh air, great scenery and health benefits – is learning about the landscapes we so often take for granted. If you want it to be, every walk can be like a detective story where you try to work out the reason why particular natural and man-made features occur – something I have enjoyed studying for years.

The Wirral landscape

The landscapes we see on Wirral, and elsewhere, do not just 'happen'. They are created by a variety of factors acting with or against each other. Man has shaped the landscape for thousands of years. It is surprising how many signs of medieval, Norse, Anglo-Saxon, Roman and even prehistoric people we can find in our area, as well as numerous signs, of course, of more recent events. To a large extent, man's activities have been driven by the local geology – the rocks and soils underfoot are constant reminders of Wirral's more distant past. And these rocks and geological conditions, together with other factors such as the weather, have combined to create a huge range of environments to support different plants and animals. I have aimed in this book to look at all these different factors and see how they have shaped the local landscape. Having said that, if there's 'too much information', just relax and enjoy the walk for its own sake.

A word about equipment

If you are not used to country walking you may be unsure what you need. My general advice is to keep it simple. Wherever you are walking on the Wirral, you are never going to be very far from civilisation. There is usually likely to be a road, track or building within a few hundred metres so there's no need to go equipped for a major expedition. And, if you do lose your way, other people will almost always be very helpful and friendly. I lost count of the number of times I was standing in a field, checking my notes and map to prepare this book, and kind people came up to me to ask if I needed directions.

My basic advice is:

Maps – carrying one is not essential on any of the routes, as the maps in the textbook should give you all the key information. Having said that I always carry an Ordnance Survey map, at 1:25,000 scale – just because it can answer lots of questions about the landscape and help clear up the occasional uncertainty. The Wirral map is no. 266 in the Explorer Range. For Walk 26, across Halkyn Mountain Common, you can use no. 265.

A compass – not usually essential, for the same reason. If you are walking in very poor visibility though, a compass and map are highly recommended. Once my wife and I did a complete 360-degree circuit of a field without realising it, in thick fog, as we didn't have a compass!

Footwear – one hazard you might need to be prepared for is mud. Many of the walks are on dry ground but on a few routes you may encounter some muddy stretches, especially if you are walking in winter and/or crossing farmland. Wirral's soil is often clay which can sometimes form sticky patches.

So if the 'Walking Conditions' at the start of each route says there may be mud then be ready for it. This means having good waterproof shoes or preferably boots. Wellies are not ideal for walking in but are often practical for shorter walks if you expect very muddy stretches, and are often best for children.

Refreshments – a bottle or two of liquid will seldom go amiss, and are certainly recommended on hot summer days. Plenty of liquid is essential for the longer routes, i.e. Halkyn Mountain and the Shore-to-Shore, and is recommended where there are no other refreshments available, e.g. on Hilbre Island. Most of the other routes can be accomplished in half a day but why not take a picnic anyway and make a day of it? In addition, a supply of sweets helps keep energy levels up – and are great motivators for reluctant children!

Clothing – wear whatever is comfortable but bear in mind that, if a walk takes two or three hours, the weather can change substantially in that time. Take waterproof jackets if rain is forecast. The Hilbre Island and Halkyn Mountain walks can be quite exposed, so have warm clothing available – the weather may be warm at home but could be cool and windy along these routes.

A walking pole (woe betide you if you say a walker is holding a 'walking stick'!): again, far from essential but having said that, I wouldn't be without mine. My wife and I stopped counting the number of uses we had put it to after about number 30. These range from testing the soundness of Scottish footbridges to retrieving maps that have blown into trees! Oh, and they take a lot of stress off your joints too.

The Countryside Code
We are lucky to enjoy such superb countryside but it takes care to keep it that way – care by landowners and by users. We all have a responsibility to look after the countryside, and the Countryside Code summarises what we should all do:

- Be safe – plan ahead and follow any signs
- Leave gates and property as you find them
- Protect plants and animals, and take your litter home
- Keep dogs under close control
- Consider other people

For more information, see the official website: www.countrysideaccess.gov.uk/countryside_code. If you want to be more involved with preserving our local footpaths then why not join the Wirral Footpaths and Open Spaces Preservation Society? Their website, www.wirralfootpaths.org.uk gives much more information.

But that's enough from me. You didn't buy this book for a long introduction – so on with the walks!

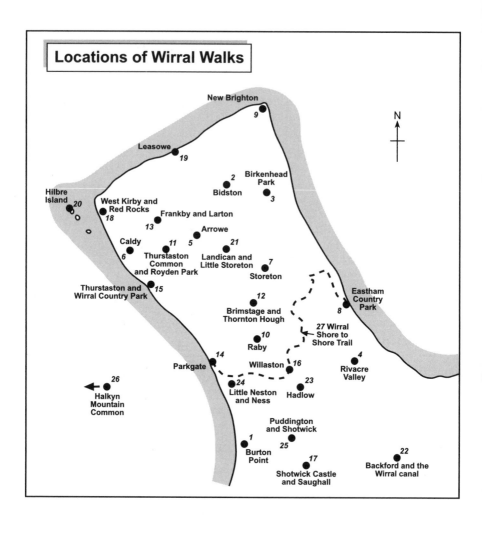

Locations of Wirral Walks

New Brighton
9

N

Leasowe
19

2 Birkenhead
Park
Bidston
3

Hilbre
Island 20
West Kirby and
Red Rocks
18
Frankby and Larton
13

Arrowe

Caldy
6
11 5
Thurstaston
Common
and Royden Park
Landican and
Little Storeton
21
7
Storeton

Thurstaston and 15
Wirral Country Park
12
Brimstage and
Thornton Hough
Eastham
Country
Park
8

27 Wirral
Shore to
Shore Trail

10
Raby

14
Parkgate
Willaston 16
4
Rivacre
Valley

26
Halkyn
Mountain
Common
24
Little Neston
and Ness
Hadlow
23

Puddington
and Shotwick
1
25
Burton
Point
17
Shotwick Castle
and Saughall
22
Backford and the
Wirral canal

Walk 1: Burton Point

**Superb scenery – an Iron Age hillfort – great birdlife – a
medieval quarry – historic engineering of the
Dee Estuary – no traffic!**

Start and finish	On the marsh-side verge on Station Road, ¾ mile west of Burton village. Burton is signposted off the A540
Distance	Just under 1½ miles
Approximate time	Allow at least an hour
Refreshments	None on the route. Ness Gardens, a short drive away, has a café and The Wheatsheaf pub is in nearby Ness
Walking conditions	Tarmac throughout. Occasionally, you may see a red flag flying at the start, warning of activity at the nearby firing range. Don't worry, you are still allowed (and safe!) to do the route, but don't wander onto the marsh. (I've seen the flag many times but have never heard firing, by the way)

This stunning walk breaks all my self-imposed rules. It's much shorter than I'd usually consider worth writing about, it's all on tarmac and it returns over exactly the same route that it goes out on. Yet it packs more points of interest than many walks ten times the length. If you are after a short, thoroughly rewarding outing you won't do better. And, for a bonus, it's completely traffic free and oh-so peaceful!

Please note, this is sheep country so it's essential that dogs are kept on a short lead at all times.

Before you start, take a look at the roadway along the coast here. Although the land looks like a natural part of the scenery, in fact it is a man-made strip built at least 200 years ago. You are parked where there was once a wide bay that extended into the lower part of what is now a large field on the other side of the road. Ten ships were anchored here in 1690. The anchorage was a source of revenue for Denhall Hospital – a religious institution founded in 1230. You can still see bumps and hollows where it stood on the left side of the field. The hospital wasn't just for the sick but provided hospital-ity for travellers as well as the poor and homeless. The buildings were demolished in the 1700s and some of the stone was used to make the field wall as well as a large local barn.

1. **From the verge, walk south to where the road bends left. Take the kissing gate on the right. Then just follow the tarmac road!**

This land, Burton Marsh, belongs to the Royal Society for the Protection of Birds, who very kindly agreed to me publishing this route. Because of the enormous diversity and quantity of birdlife that the Dee Estuary attracts, the area has been given the highest designation for a natural site – a Site of Special Scientific Interest. You are likely to see many types of bird along the route – for more information or membership visit the nearby RSPB office (300 metres up Station Road at present; moving to Puddington Lane, Burton in 2011).

After 500 metres or so you pass sheep dips and pens on your left. Opposite is a large stand of common reed – the type used in thatching roofs. They are home to several kinds of warblers, as well as reed buntings, in summer and spring.

You are walking along a road that used to lead to the Shotton Steelworks but it was closed many years ago. The white lines you'll see in the centre of the road seem very strange in this traffic-free setting.

After a while you notice outcrops of sandstone to your left and then the lengthy face of a quarry. Sandstone has been taken from here for centuries for use in buildings, field walls and the embankment discussed below.

2. **Stop when you reach a rise in the road. This is the best spot to look for Flint Castle which is believed to have been made from**

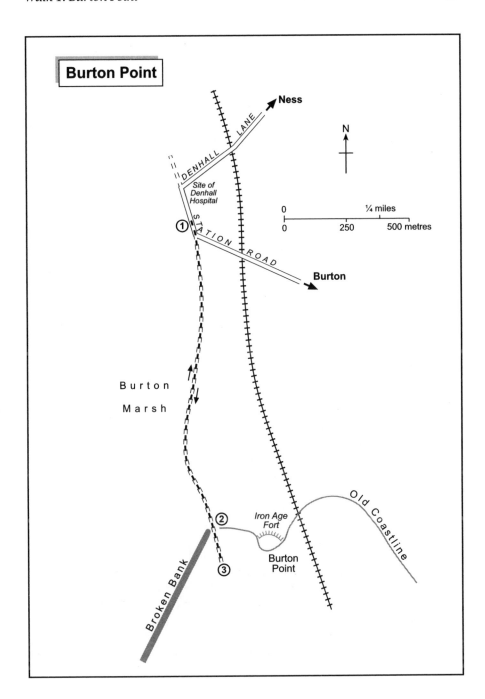

Burton Point

Ness

Site of Denhall Hospital

Burton

N

0   ¼ miles
0   250   500 metres

Burton Marsh

Iron Age Fort

Old Coastline

Broken Bank

Burton Point

quarried Burton stone in 1278. How easy it is for you to see depends upon the weather and time of day – to help, look across to the top of the high ground in Wales and find a group of about five pylons in a slight dip. Drop your gaze to the estuary shore below this point and you will (hopefully) make out the curved, brown towers of the castle.

The rise in the road here is due to an embankment which runs roughly south-west from this point, across the marsh. For centuries, shifting sands meant that the Dee was hard to navigate, especially for large ships bringing goods destined for Chester. So, in 1737 the course was diverted from a point near Neston to the other side of the estuary, and partly canalised. A number of embankments were built over the following 180 years to prevent flooding and to reclaim the land for agricultural use. This embankment, known as Broken Bank, was built in the 1880s and would have been made using the locally quarried stone.

Burton Point, the site of an Iron Age fort

Go forward a few metres, dropping to get a good view of the tree-capped hill to your left – Burton Point. On this hill are the remains of an Iron Age hillfort – the only one on Wirral and built between about 800 BC and 43 AD It consists of a ditch and bank that would probably originally have run across a neck of land (so, technically, it is a 'promontory fort'). However subsequent quarrying has removed much of the land and the fort's earthworks so we will never know its exact original size and shape. People may have lived within its boundaries or maybe just used it as a place of refuge. It has been archaeologically surveyed and is believed to have been linked to the trade in Cheshire salt. (Please don't try to clamber over to the fort as there is no access. The land is private and legally protected but the RSPB do organise guided walks there from time to time.)

The headland of Burton Point provided a place of shelter for ships along the English shore of the estuary. It was being used as early as the 1300s, when Burton was a market town, and was still a place for ships to unload goods 400 years later. Today – a little ironically – a railway line runs through the area where ships once anchored. Beyond the line, but out of sight, RSPB-owned wetlands provide a sanctuary for freshwater-loving birds.

3. **Turn round and retrace your steps, enjoying the tranquility and the fabulous open views to the mouth of the estuary.**

Walk 2: Bidston

**Giraffe food – woodland and heath – a windmill –
a children's farm – ancient rock carvings –
maritime history – old buildings**

Start and finish	Car park by Tam O'Shanter Urban Farm, signposted off the B5151, Boundary Road
Distance	1¾ or 2¼ miles
Approximate time	Allow at least 1½ hours, plus time at the farm
Refreshments	At Tam O'Shanter's Farm
Walking conditions	Woodland and heathland paths – mostly dry but occasional muddy patches after rain, which are usually easy to avoid; some uneven, rocky surfaces. One optional short climb

This is a short walk, but allow plenty of time as there's so much to see around this lovely area of heath and woodland.

Start with a visit to Tam O'Shanter Urban Farm – open daily from 9.30 to 4.30, free of charge. There are plenty of animals (the ducks live in 'Duckingham Palace'!) as well as an interesting activity room, a Treasure Hunt course and a Nature Trail. Take time to look at the thatched cottage, with its stone carving of Tam O'Shanter fleeing from a witch across a bridge. Also the new Ecobuilding, which has walls made of straw bales, solar panels and a roof covered with the succulent plant 'sedum'. The rainwater that falls on it is filtered and used to flush the toilets – an example of 'greywater recycling'.

1. **Take the track marked 'Permissive Horseride to Upton Road' between the car park and the entrance to the Farm.**

2. **At a wide path turn right for 50 metres; then turn left,**

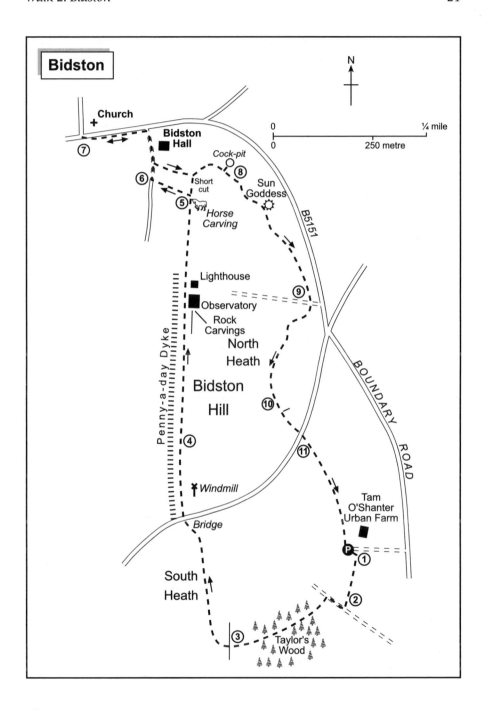

immediately after the picnic bench, to enter the wood. After a few metres fork right, to go through the centre of the wood.

This is Taylor's Wood, a 9-hectare woodland. It has a lovely feeling of openness, and is dominated by Scots Pine, with its characteristic red bark higher up the trunk. You are sure to see grey squirrels scurrying around.

3. **Go past the left-hand end of an old stone wall, continuing ahead, almost immediately, onto a path of exposed sandstone. Bend right towards the windmill, eventually crossing a bridge to reach the mill.**

From the wood you enter an area of heathland. Heath is characterised by thin soil, lacking in nutrients. Typical plants include common heather (as well as other types of heather), spiky gorse whose yellow flowers have a characteristic coconut smell, and silver birch. In fact, birch is so abundant here that some of it is cut and crushed, and then used to feed giraffes at Chester Zoo!

At wetter times of the year there are ponds along this stretch where you may spot large grey herons.

The windmill was built around 1800. It replaced one that burnt down when a gale turned the sails too fast, causing friction that started a fire. It is usually open to the public on some Saturdays in the summer, but is closed in the winter to avoid disturbing brown long-eared bats which nest there.

Bidston Mill

The old mill was situated 30 metres north of the current one (by the second bench after the windmill) and was rotated into the wind by the miller pushing on a wooden arm sticking out near the base. Two oblongs you can see carved in the rock were anchor points for the brake of the mill's turning mechanism; 3 metres further north are carved footholds used by the miller to help him push the wooden arm. A Bidston miller was once killed when he stepped out of the mill and was hit by one of the sails (which were longer than those seen today). On another occasion a tinker's donkey that was tethered to a sail flew into the air when the sail rotated – it survived!

5 metres later, on the opposite side of the path, there is a round post-hole in the rock. This was one of sixty two on the ridge, used from the 1760s, to hold poles for flags giving news to Liverpool merchants of incoming ships so they could get ready for unloading. Later, a series of high-level semaphore signal-stations was established at Bidston, Hilbre and along the north Wales coast – messages could be passed along the chain of signal-stations from Anglesey to Liverpool in eight minutes. Further along the ridge you will be able to see the view down the coast, to the Great Orme (by Llandudno) 55 miles away.

4. **Continue along the ridge to Bidston Observatory.**

Immediately before the Observatory you may like to drop down the steps by the wall. To your right is a vertical face of sandstone on which you can find carvings of two human figures and a horse.

There used to be an astronomical telescope in each of the Observatory's two rotating domes. Later, it became the Liverpool Observatory and Tidal Institute, calculating tide times around the world and inventing the first electric tide-predicting machine. The Institute played a key role in predicting tides for the World War II D-Day landings in France. Now the site is disused and, at the time of writing, its fate is unknown.

The wall to your left is called Penny-a-day Dyke and was built 600 years ago as part of the boundary of a deer park which stretched down towards the River Fender. Its builders were paid one old penny (about ½p) per day.

This lighthouse was built in 1872 but is no longer in use. This, and its predecessor, was used in conjunction with Leasowe Lighthouse

(Walk 19); when the two were in alignment it indicated the entrance for ships to the Rock Channel which led towards Liverpool's docks.

Just before point 5 you walk over an area of flat sandstone. Take a few moments to study it and you will make out a carving of a horse – it was once 3.5 metres long but is being increasingly worn down and now only the head is really clear. Its origin is unknown.

5. **Follow the path as it turns left and drops downhill. (For the short cut, continue straight ahead, passing a stone gatepost to your right, along a narrow path overgrown with holly and rhododendrons. Emerge between points 7 and 8.)**

6. **At the bottom of the hill, turn right to visit Bidston village, a Conservation Area.**

You pass a huge millstone at the entrance to Bidston Hall Farm Mews (the stone is not from the local windmills but is of similar size). On the right is Bidston Hall, probably built in the early 1600s. Not only is the grey sandstone building impressive but it also has a magnificent raised gateway. The Hall is said to have once been lost and won in a game of cards; a summerhouse was subsequently built in the shape of the ace of clubs.

There are many fascinating buildings in the village made from the same local stone. These include Lilac Cottages on the right, with tiny windows; and, opposite, Yew tree Farm, dated 1697; Stone Farm (by the letterbox) – a former inn known as the Ring O' Bells, which was linked to a local smuggling network; and Church Farm on your left, which has 13 different floor levels inside (indicated by the many different levels of windows you can see).

7. **Retrace your steps and at the corner of the wall after Bidston Hall take a narrow path uphill – it winds a little but basically runs alongside the wall of the Hall's garden. Towards the top of the hill, where paths cross, turn left and continue ahead.**

After about 75 metres look for a short path on your left just after a bank with an oak tree on it. This leads to a circular area called the "Cock-pit". Its origins are uncertain but it may have once been a mill for grinding gorse for animal feed; it is thought to have then become a site where illegal cockfights took place.

8. **Retrace your steps and continue along the path.**

By the house, look for a wooden post marking the Sun Goddess, arms outstretched, which is carved into a flat piece of sandstone. She faces exactly east, towards the rising sun on midsummer's day, and is thought to have been carved by Norse settlers around 1000 years ago.

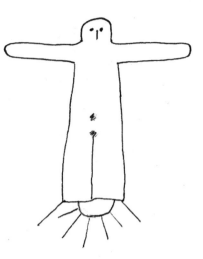

The Sun Godess

Continue on the main path downhill, ignoring paths to the left, eventually reaching a fork where you bear right, slightly uphill.

9. **Cross the tarmac drive that leads to the Observatory, to pick up the narrow path starting about three metres to your right up the drive. Soon, come to an old metal fence and continue with it on your left, keeping as close as the path allows.**

10. **At a break in a ruined wall, go left to drop downhill.**

11. **Cross the road. After 100m, go left at a wooden fence to take the path back to the car park.**

Walk 3: Birkenhead Park

A pretty and historic park – wildlife, including wildfowl to feed – unusual buildings – a link to New York

Start and finish	Corner of Park Road East and Park Road North (A553), Birkenhead
Distance	2 or 2¾ miles
Approximate time	1½ or 2 hours
Refreshments	Café at the Park Pavilion
Walking conditions	Level paths throughout, suitable for wheelchairs, pushchairs etc.

If you are not familiar with Birkenhead Park, you might be surprised by its story and the variety of its scenery. If you do know it, you will already appreciate how it offers a little oasis of tranquility in the urban sprawl of Birkenhead and its surroundings. Either way it offers the opportunity for a gentle stroll with plenty to see. If you have children, taking bread to feed the birds on the lakes – including swans, moorhens and mallard ducks – it is a 'must'!

You'll notice that the parkland is generally very flat. This is because, until the 1840s, this area was just marshland. However, prompted by a government initiative to create better recreational facilities for people in the growing towns of England, a local man, William Jackson, had the visionary idea of creating a park for the public's use. Nowadays we take parks for granted, but making a purpose-built publicly funded park that anyone could use was a new idea in early Victorian England.

1. **Go through The Grand Entrance, with its 12 columns and 1847 datestone, made from sandstone quarried at Storeton (Walk 7). Continue ahead to the Jackson Monument, dedicated to the brother of the man who was the driving force behind the Park.**

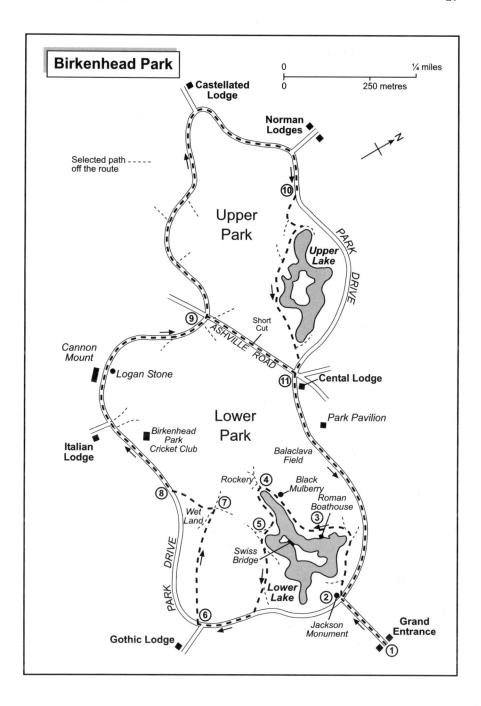

Birkenhead Park

0 ¼ miles

0 250 metres

Selected path - - - - -
off the route

Castellated
Lodge

Norman
Lodges

Upper
Park

Upper
Lake

PARK DRIVE

ASHVILLE ROAD

Short
Cut

⑨

Cannon
Mount

Logan Stone

⑪ Cental Lodge

Park Pavilion

Lower
Park

Birkenhead
Park
Cricket Club

Italian
Lodge

⑧

Balaclava
Field

Rockery ④

Black
Mulberry

Roman
Boathouse
③

Wet
Land

⑦

⑤

PARK DRIVE

Swiss
Bridge

Lower
Lake

②

⑥

Jackson
Monument

Grand
Entrance

Gothic Lodge

①

⑩

2. **Go right for 10 metres, then left to pick up the lakeside path, going anti-clockwise.**

This path constantly curves, as do most of the other paths, and the banks of the three lakes. The designer of the park, Sir Joseph Paxton, wanted to create a 'countryside' feel with open meadows, meandering waters and scattered trees. Just as in nature, you will find few straight lines here.

There are likely to be fishermen around the lake – it holds many types of fish including pike, roach, bream, carp, perch and tench.

3. **Reach the Roman Boathouse, which once held rowing boats for hire. Climb the steps and admire the pebble mosaic floor, laid in 1990.**

Continue, and after a few metres you will see the brightly coloured Swiss Bridge to your left. It was inaccessible for many years but

The Lower Lake

you can access it now (before point 5 below), following a recent £11.4 million two-year restoration of the park and its facilities.

Continue along the path and look for a wide grassy gap between the trees to your right. Immediately after this gap, on a bank about 3 metres away from the path, is a 'black mulberry' tree with its distinctive gnarled, reddish-brown trunk. In late summer, the tree produces mulberries, which are similar to raspberries, and which you will find scattered all over the path. Next time you sing the nursery rhyme 'Here we go round the mulberry bush ...', you'll be able to picture one!

4. **Continue to a junction of paths to find the rockery, made of sandstone slabs and popular with clambering children.**

The park's designer, Paxton, dug the lakes and used them to drain off some of the water from the marsh on which the park was built. He used the material excavated from the lakes to form the small hills throughout the park, which break up the flat landscape.

In 1850, three years after the Park opened, Frederick Olmsted visited it. He went on to design Central Park in New York and said he drew many of his ideas from Birkenhead.

5. **Stay on the lakeside path, taking a short diversion after a while to visit the Swiss Bridge. A few metres later keep left at a grassy mound between a triangle of paths. Continue ahead, ignoring paths to the left, to reach the perimeter road – Park Drive. Go right.**

Horse-drawn carriages once paraded along this wide track, leaving the inner parts of the Park safe for pedestrians.

In the corner of the Park note the first of six Lodges, built in different architectural styles. This is the 'Gothic Lodge', made of pale sandstone blocks and with octagonal chimneys.

Turn right, down the narrower path between lime trees.
6.
Limes can live up to 500 years but these were planted in 1953 to mark Queen Elizabeth's coronation.

Continue to a cross-paths in a slight dip.

7. **Go left. After a few metres, there is a small lake to your left.**

   This is Figure of Eight Lake. Fed by a spring and originally intended as the park's third lake, it had difficulties retaining water and became a shallow, marshy, wetland. It has now been re-created as a nature area with an island and a platform for educational studies.

8. **Continue ahead reaching Park Drive, and pass the tented pavilions of Birkenhead Park Cricket Club.**

   The pavilion was opened in 1993. Creating areas for people to play sports was part of the grand plan for the Park from the start. Birkenhead Cricket Club was formed in 1846, in anticipation of the opening of the Park.

The Castellated Lodge

100 metres after the pavilion you can see the impressive 'Italian Lodge' by the gates to your left with its nine-arched viewing tower.

Soon, at the top of a gentle rise, you see a pillar – the Logan Stone – marking the holding here of the 1917 Welsh National Eisteddfod (there was once a large Welsh-speaking community each side of the Mersey). Interestingly this stone, placed in England to mark a Welsh festival, is made of granite from.......Scotland!

On your left immediately before the Logan Stone is a large property, Cannon Mount, one of many Victorian properties around the Park's edge. When the Park was created, about 40 hectares (100 acres) of perimeter land was set aside for building plots, the sale price of which more than paid for the Park's construction.

The Victorian pillar box near the Central Lodge

9. **Reach Ashville Road. Turn right for the shorter walk, otherwise cross the road into the Upper Park which tends to be quieter than Lower Park, where you have been. Stay on Park Drive to reach the 'Castellated Lodge' with its castle-like features. Continuing on the main track, you pass the two 'Norman Lodges' after about 250 metres, standing each side of another gated entrance.**

75 metres later fork right onto a narrower path and take the first path left to reach another lakeside path. Turn right i.e. go anti-clockwise round the lake.

Along here on your left you pass a fat, bulbous, blackened tree – a sweet chestnut with deep, twisting bark furrows– which looks like something out of Harry Potter!

10. **Fork right near the end to reach another gated entrance and cross Ashville Road again (note the unusual hexagonal pillar box to your left, the scrolled 'VR' letters indicating it is Victorian) and pass the 'Central Lodge'.**

11. **Continue on Park Drive back to the start.**

To your right, by the children's play area, is Balaclava Field, named after the famous battle in the 1850s' Crimean War when the Charge of the Light Brigade occurred. Two Russian cannon captured in the war once stood on Cannon Hill. Nowadays, at weekends, 'battle' takes place here between football teams, with just the occasional scuffle breaking out!

You will pass a new Park Pavilion on your left. It houses a café, information point, toilets and gallery, and is the base or meeting point for many of the park's events and activities. Its design is reminiscent of a palm house, the glass front offering unobstructed views out over the formal flower garden into the park.

Walk 4: Rivacre Valley

Woodland – a one-time major tourist attraction – wildflower meadows – wildlife – wood carvings

Start and finish	Rivacre Valley local Nature Reserve on the B5132, between junctions 6 and 7 of the M53
Distance	2 miles or 3½ miles
Approximate time	Allow 1 hour or 2 hours
Refreshments	Ellesmere Port Golf Centre open to non-members most days for drinks
Walking conditions	Generally easy walking, often on firm paths. Some woodland stretches may be muddy after rain

This corner of Wirral is often overlooked, but this is a lovely walk through several deciduous woodlands, besides streams, and down a meadowy valley that feels miles from anywhere. If you want to see the cornflower meadow at its best, try to visit from mid-summer to mid-autumn.

Rivacre Valley Local Nature Reserve covers over 160 hectares (400 acres) and forms part of The Mersey Forest – an initiative covering large parts of north Cheshire and Merseyside creating new green spaces, woodlands, ponds, hedges and meadows.

1. **Take the path to the right of the rangers' cabin, and turn left at the top of the steps. Continue ahead when a path joins from the right.**

The area to your right once offered an attraction of national interest – an outdoor swimming pool set in beautifully landscaped rose gardens. People flocked from far and wide to bathe in the Olympic-sized pool, opened in 1934, which was filled by water pumped from the Manchester Ship Canal a mile away. It closed in 1981 and the hole was infilled leaving no sign today. (You can see photos in the rangers' cabin if it is open.) Look out for a rectangular concrete area along this path, about 10m before a badger carving on a log – there are several holes where metal pipes once emerged, probably into a shower block.

2. **At the path T-junction, turn left. Continue straight ahead with houses on your right. When the path swings right, go straight ahead, across grass, with trees to your left. At the end of the trees take the faint path that drops downhill.**

To your right is Cornfield Meadow which is managed to create a wonderful patchwork of wildflowers, attracting a range of insects and butterflies. It is ploughed in winter, with wildflower seed sown in spring to produce beautiful meadowland in mid-summer to mid-autumn. There is an interpretation board by the metal fence on the far side of the meadow that tells you about the flowers.

3. **At the bottom of the hill, turn left onto the tarmac path. Just before metal gates turn right down another path.**

4. **At the bottom of this hill, fork right and cross a metal footbridge over Rivacre Brook to enter Well Wood. A few metres later turn left on a gravel path.**

If you look into the area of woodland by the path here – you may be able to see that many of the hazel bushes have been coppiced (but these aren't always easy to see if coppicing has taken place only recently; it last happened in 2009). Under this ancient practice selected types of trees and bushes are cut back to their base, typically every seven years. This encourages new growth in the form of several shoots rising from the stump to make straight and sturdy poles. These have many uses including fencing.

In spring this area is carpeted with bluebells.

Well Wood is named after St. Helen's Well which was one of three wells situated in the wood. The building foundations you pass on the right once housed one of the wells, used by Bowaters paper

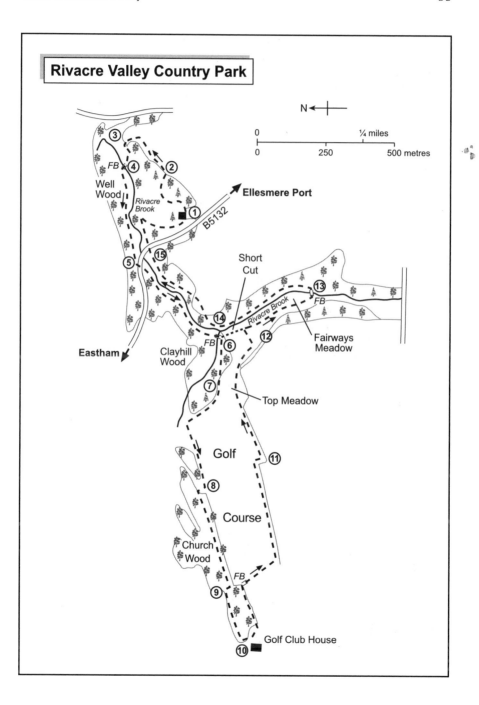

Rivacre Valley Country Park

manufacturers to supply water to their nearby factory. Another, surviving, example of the building can be found at the road.

5. **Cross the road (Take care! Traffic can be fast here). Go right for a few metres, then through a wooden barrier, to join a tarmac path through Clayhill Wood. Continue to a bridge made of railway sleepers, crossing it.**

Clayhill Wood, like Well Wood, is an area of semi-natural ancient woodland which means that is has existed for many centuries, managed by man, for

Bullrushes

example by coppicing. Today this stretch seems to be a favourite with children and dogs who love splashing around in the brook.

Keep an eye open for little birds bobbing their tails up and down as they stand by the water – some pairs of yellow wagtails thrive along the brook. And about 20m before the bridge, just by a fallen willow spanning the brook, you may be able to spot several small holes in the far side of the stream bank. These are kingfisher nests and, if you are very lucky, you may get a glimpse of this iridescent blue bird darting along the brook.

6. **A few metres later, at cross-paths turn right to go uphill. (For the shorter walk, continue straight ahead at the cross-paths to enter a valley; go to point 12 below).**

7. **A few metres after the bench near the top of the hill fork right along a grassy path to reach a golf course. Keep to the right-hand edge of the course, through a gap in a chain-link fence. Stay on the good path for 40m to a hedge and turn left to walk with the ditch on your right.**

8. **Ignore the first crossing over the ditch, but take a second one on a good path, shortly after a group of willows in a hollow. However don't follow the path round to the right but go straight ahead into woodland through overhanging trees (it doesn't look promising, but bear with me!). A few metres in, pick up the obvious path to go left through Church Wood.**

This is a lovely path but beware of tree roots which present plenty of trip hazards!

9. **The path eventually swings right and comes to a path-junction. Turn left and continue straight ahead between ponds to right and left, through woodland.**

The ponds are marl pits – see page 168.

Eventually you come to the wall of the churchyard of the large and ornate St Paul's Church, Hooton (you can get a view through the gate on your right; note also the map on a boulder here).

10. **For refreshments go straight ahead to the golf centre. Otherwise turn hard left by the churchyard gate and boulder, almost doubling back on yourself. Join a gravel path at the end of a small open area, re-entering the wood. 150 metres later go right to cross a bridge which is made of railway sleepers. Continue straight head, going over the golf course, passing ponds, and keeping in the same direction to reach a fence corner. Turn left, and follow the path, which eventually turns sharp right.**

Just before the sharp right-hand bend, on your left on the golf course, are two sandstone blocks below oak trees – they look like old boundary stones but I haven't yet worked out what the lettering carved on them stands for.

11. **Reach a cul de sac – but go left, staying on the wooded path. Later, just after a wooden barrier/entrance on the right, take a grassy path that forks to the right, swinging away from the golf course and along the right-hand edge of the grassy space of Top Meadow. At the red brick wall, continue ahead.**

Fairways Meadow

12. **After about 75m, when the view opens up to the left, drop down the wide break in vegetation to reach the valley bottom. Turn right.**

On your right you pass a totem pole decorated with various symbols relating to Ellesmere Port including the 'Mersey Forest' tree, the emblems of major local companies Shell and Vauxhall, and a whale which represents one that the pole's carver once rescued from the Mersey!

This lovely valley is managed as hay meadow. It is called Fairways, giving away the fact that it once formed part of a golf course. The meadow is cut late each year after the seeds of the flowers and grasses have fallen, ready to provide next year's growth.

13. **Walk for about 250m then look for a path forking left, over a footbridge. Cross, and turn left again to walk alongside Rivacre Brook.**

In places where the bank is eroding you may see barriers woven from local sticks of willow. The sticks of willow continue to live after being taken from the parent tree and planted in the mud, to make 'living fences'.

14. **Later at a footbridge, do not cross but turn right, staying on the main path. Go past a metal barrier and 10m later fork left into a small clearing, passing right of a picnic bench. Pick up the path on the opposite side of the clearing. Follow it to the road.**

15. **Go straight across the road; after 200m take a tarmac path forking right and soon go right again uphill. Continue back to the car park.**

Around you as you climb the hill is the 'International Woodland', younger than the earlier ancient woodland and made up of trees donated by many countries worldwide. Stop on the hill to admire the superbly carved wooden seat – how many types of animal, bird or insect can you count?

Walk 5: Arrowe Country Park

Waterfalls – wildlife – parkland – woodland – sites of historic interest

Start and finish	Car Park on Arrowe Brook Road (which branches off the A551 between Arrowe Park Hospital and Sainsbury's)
Distance	2¼ or 3½ miles
Approximate time	Allow 1½ or 2 hours
Refreshments	Cherry Orchard pub at the park's main entrance, and at Arrowe Park Golf Centre
Walking conditions	Grass, tarmac, woodland paths, fields. Can occasionally be muddy after rain in places, but the part most likely to be muddy – Gorse Covert – can be avoided by using the tarmac track from the car park to point 3

Arrowe is one of Britain's largest public parks – 172 hectares (425 acres), making it bigger than Hyde Park in London. It has many amenities and you may also see model aircraft being put through their paces after point 2. Much of this walk is through deciduous woodland and it makes a fine route at any time of year, with varying leaf colour through the seasons and changing bird and animal life.

In 1985 the park was the scene of a much-publicised incident when the South-African-born runner, Zola Budd, was bundled out of the Women's National Cross Country Championships by protestors, injuring her jaw. Budd, a top 3,000-metre runner, had controversially been given British citizenship so she could represent Britain in the 1984 Los Angeles Olympics (sports' fans may recall that she came seventh in the Olympics after accidentally tripping up American favourite Mary Decker).

1. **At the far end of the car park go though a gap in the wooden fence and go straight ahead to the wooded area. Go left, along its edge, until you find the first clear path on your right, by a wooden post.**

2. **Go through the woodland, Gorse Covert. When you emerge, cross the gravel path, and aim slightly left towards higher ground, right of the hospital buildings, to walk alongside a line of trees.**

The trees are white poplars and the little diamond shapes on the bark are typical of them. When the trees are in leaf, they seem to shimmer in the breeze.

The large open area around you was the scene of the 1929 Boy Scout Jamboree, attended by Baden-Powell, the founder of the scout movement (who found out he was to be *Lord* Baden-Powell while the Jamboree was in progress). This was the 'Coming of Age Jamboree' as the movement was 21 years old, and 50,000 scouts came from 50 countries. There was a large central arena surrounded by a sea of tents one mile long. At the end of the meeting, Baden-Powell sent a message of peace from Arrowe, via his scouts, all over the world. From then on, the Golden *Arrow* became the Scout symbol of peace.

3. **Join the main tarmac path. Ignore the path to the left, towards a modern building, but continue on the main path which soon bends left. You reach an old toilet block and 75 metres later, at a 5-way crossing, turn right, soon reaching Arrowe Hall to your right.**

The Hall was built in 1835 by John Shaw, a member of a wealthy ship-owning family which had made money from slave trading through Liverpool. The Hall was later enlarged to exhibit trophies, including nine tigers, from one family member's hunting expeditions. The building became a hospital during both world wars.

Opposite Arrowe Hall the tall conifers on your left are giant redwood trees. Touch the bark and you will find it is soft and spongy – not what you might expect from such mighty giants. In

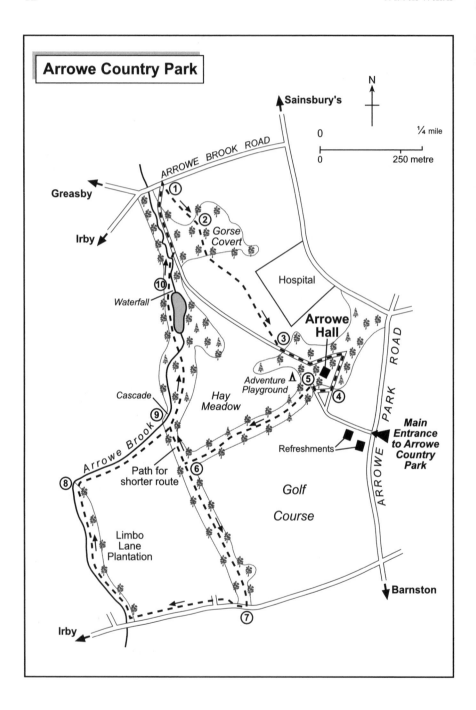

total, the park has 43 tree species, many rare, including four types of oak – pedunculate, sessile, turkey and red.

The land was later owned by Lord Leverhulme (who built Port Sunlight) who gave it to Birkenhead Corporation in 1926 for the 'enjoyment of the public'.

4 **Soon after the hall, at another cross-paths just before a low metal fence on the left, turn right. Turn right again at the next junction a few metres later and soon enter the woodland.**

5. **Cross a wooden footbridge; go immediately left onto a path through the wood. (Children will prefer you to first go ahead, to the nearby play area!)**

There are ponds on both sides in this woodland. These are old marl pits – turn to page 168 for more information.

At the first track crossing the path take a short detour to the right to the stone gateposts. On the grassland there are some more, isolated, stone posts standing on the grass. When John Shaw, Mayor of Liverpool, bought the land in 1800 it was farmland and these surviving gateposts are left over from that time. In certain light you may also be able to see dips and troughs in the field – probably signs of old 'ridge and furrow' farming (see pages 95-6).

Return to the main path and take a similar detour at the next crossing track (but no gate posts this time).

The grassland here is managed as hay meadow. No pesticides are used, allowing natural

A sandstone pillar left from when the park was farmland

growth of flowers and grasses. Each half is usually cut in summer in alternate years, with the other half left to grow to provide habitats for over-wintering animal life. You may see a kestrel hovering over the meadow, waiting to swoop on some unsuspecting vole or mouse.

To your left is the golf course whose ponds include the rare great-crested newt. The range of wild animals and plants is the reason why much of the park has been designated a 'Site of Biological Interest' (SBI).

6. **You eventually meet another path. For the shorter walk turn right at this junction to reach point 9. Otherwise, go straight ahead, over a footbridge and across decking, at the end of which immediately turn left, keeping on the path within the woodland.**

Note how this plantation has a healthy mix of trees of various ages.

The lake at Arrowe Country Park

The numerous narrow ridges and dips were made when the trees were first planted, and would have assisted drainage.

Birds to keep an eye open for here include great spotted woodpeckers (if you don't see them you might hear their loud, rapid tapping as they bore into tree trunks); brightly coloured jays, nuthatches and treecreepers (nuthatches cling onto trunks and walk spirally downwards; treecreepers walk spirally up). Grey squirrels are everywhere!

7. **Continue to a road, turning right along it for 600m (ignore the permissive route to the right shortly after Parkway). When the service road ends, at a small turning circle, turn right, signed to Arrowe Brook Lane, walking alongside Arrowe Brook through Limbo Lane Plantation.**

8. **The path eventually goes over a footbridge over the brook but turn right immediately *before* this, through a metal gate, signed 'Permissive Footpath'.**

9. **After three more gates you re-enter woodland. Go down and up the steps, then straight ahead to reach the main path after 25m. You will want to go left, but before you do …**

There is a lovely little water cascade on your left here. In summer it is just a trickle but, when it's wet, the water tumbles and splashes noisily down little natural sandstone steps. Keep an eye out for kingfishers along this streamside section – they are more likely to be seen if you are an early morning walker.

Continue, eventually reaching a lake.

The lake, now popular with anglers after carp and bream, was made by the Shaw family who dammed Arrowe Brook. At the far end is a man-made waterfall (though if the weather's dry the water will not be doing much falling!).

10. **Continue along the path you have been on, to join a tarmac one which takes you back to the car park.**

Walk 6: Caldy

Heathland – fine views – a pretty village – a beach

Start and finish	Wirral Country Park car park near the bottom of Croft Drive, Caldy (to find it, from the A540 Telegraph Road follow the signs to Caldy; fork left after the church down Croft Drive. Go first right, continuing to the bottom of the hill; the car park is on your right)
Distance	About 2½ miles
Approximate time	Allow 1½ hours
Refreshments	Two bars/pubs towards the end of the route
Walking conditions	Dry, sometimes uneven, paths, which may occasionally be overgrown with prickly plants

This short walk takes in pretty Caldy village and the nearby fine lowland heath, as well as offering superb views. You may also like to visit Caldy Hill National Trust reserve, with more fine views, off the B5141 Caldy Road. Before you start you may wish to look at the notice board in the car park which has a map, local information and tide times.

1. **From the car park entrance, turn left. Ignore Croft Drive West to the left but continue uphill and, as the road bends right, fork left by a telegraph pole up the signed bridleway.**

   The sandy conditions are typical of much of the walk, which is on sandstone. The stone, found in various shades, is used in local buildings, walls and The Mariners' Beacon that we will see later.

Caldy Village

2. **At the road, turn right and follow the main road through Caldy village.**

The name 'Caldy' probably comes from old Norse words meaning 'cold islands' referring to a time when this area was included in the same administrative region as the Hilbre islands. Norsemen settled on Wirral shortly after AD900.

Carved stones date several buildings to the late 1600s and early 1700s. I particularly like the 1683 Manor Farm (opposite the clock tower), made from huge sandstone blocks, covered by a sagging slate roof. In the 1830s, a wealthy Manchester businessman, Richard Barton, set about renovating local properties, creating today's 'chocolate box' village centre. He built huge Caldy Manor, complete with clock tower, which you may hear chime.

3. **Just before no. 109, Caldecot Cottage, turn left up the bridleway.**

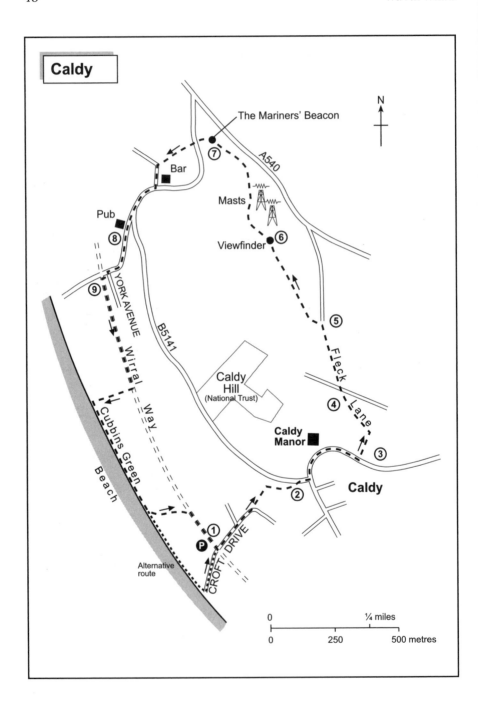

Caldy

The Mariners' Beacon

N

A540

⑦

Bar

Masts

Pub

Viewfinder ● ⑥

⑧

YORK AVENUE

⑨

B5141

⑤

Fleck

Wirral

Caldy
Hill
(National Trust)

Way

Lane

④

Cubbins Green

Caldy
Manor

Beach

③

②

Caldy

①

P

CROFT DRIVE

Alternative
route

0   ¼ miles

0   250   500 metres

4. **At the road, cross and continue almost straight ahead, to the right of a telegraph pole.**

   This old path from Caldy is called Fleck Lane. There is a great variety of young deciduous trees here, encouraging plenty of songbirds throughout the year.

5. **Stay on the walled route until 25m before the distinctive metal pole to the left of the path (and a white house shortly after it on the right). Go left through the break in the wall and follow the clear path ahead, through rhododendrons.**

   When you reach the edge of the open heathland continue ahead, on the obvious path. Keep on this path. (Numerous paths criss-cross the heath, which can occasionally be misleading if you are following directions. As general guidance, stick to the main path; aim for the wireless masts which you will see after a while, and then the tall column with the ball on top).

   Caldy Hill is an area of lowland heath. This type of habitat is threatened in the UK so the hill is very important and is designated a Site of Biological Interest. Heathland soils are typically poor in nutrients and only certain plants can put up with these conditions.

   Three types of heather are found locally, the commonest is ling with flowers on long, loose spikes; there is also bell heather which has cluster of large bell-shaped flowers on the upper stems, and cross-leaved heather, found in wetter areas, with leaves that form a cross-shape when viewed from above.

   You may also see clumps of bright green-leaved rhododendrons growing on the open heath. They can be bad news! They are not a native British plant and have a habit of overwhelming everything around them so that the natural heathland plants, and the animals they support, disappear. Serious cutting back is needed from time to time to stop them getting out of hand.

   After 350m you will see a viewfinder mounted on a stone plinth to your left.

You are 79 metres above sea level here and the viewfinder is an excellent guide to the superb views. On a clear day, you can see Anglesey (47 miles away) and even Snaefell mountain on the Isle of Man (81 miles). If you look in the indicated direction of the Snowdonia range in late autumn to early spring you may be able to spot snow-capped peaks. Hilbre Island is visible to your half-right and, beyond it, the 30 wind turbines of the North Hoyle array, Britain's first major offshore wind farm. The 25 turbines of the Rhyl Flats wind farm may also be visible further along the coast.

6. **From the viewfinder, don't go back to the path you were on. Instead take the path from the viewfinder, past a bench, going to the left of the corner of a wall, and dropping a little. Keep on the same general heading, sticking to the obvious path ahead, ignoring paths to your left and, occasionally, right. Eventually reach the Mariners' Beacon.**

Erected in 1841 as a navigation aid for shipping, this replaced a windmill that seafarers had found an invaluable landmark until it was destroyed in a storm 1839. The granite millstone at the base of the column came from the mill.

7. **Go down the steps in front of the Mariners' Beacon. At the road go straight over, alongside a fence. At the next road turn left and, at the road junction, turn right.**

8. **Immediately after the Moby Dick pub, turn right down Sandy Lane, and soon use the zebra crossing. 100m later, at York Avenue, descend the steps ahead and turn left, along the Wirral Way.**

The Wirral Way was opened in 1973, and was Britain's first designated Country Park.

The Mariners' Beacon

Previously it was a railway line, opened in 1886, enabling Victorian folk to start taking day trips to the seaside – this was long before the era of motor cars. It also made it easier to get locally produced goods to the towns and cities, including milk, grain and vegetables. The line closed to passengers in 1956, and all other traffic in 1962.

9. **After 500m, when the housing to the right ends and you get an open view across the estuary, descend the wooden-railed path and continue ahead, across Cubbins Green, to reach the cliff top. Turn left. Stay on the same heading, and enjoy the views. Eventually the path swings back onto the Wirral Way, taking you back to the car park.**

   (As an alternative, provided the tide allows, you can descend to the beach from Cubbins Green, and walk back that way. Later, climb some steps and a metal-railed path, to reach the road to the car park).

For information on the birds in the estuary, see Walk 20.

Walk 7: Storeton

**Dinosaurs! – an old tramway line – quarrying – Roman
connections – the Forest of Wirral – harsh penalties for
law breaking – a former racecourse – woodland**

Start and finish	Rough ground by the black and white footpath sign in the centre of Storeton. Storeton is signposted off the A5151, Mount Road, leading from the M53, junction 4
Distance	2½ miles
Approximate time	Allow 1½ hours (or a little more with the optional diversion)
Refreshments	None on the route but the Travellers Rest pub is at the top of Rest Hill Road by Storeton Wood
Walking conditions	Good tracks, roads; short sections of field-paths

*This gentle walk offers fine views over central Wirral and goes through
the delightful Storeton Wood. This area was the site of stone quarrying
for centuries and examples of Storeton stone engraved by the Romans
can be seen in Chester Grosvenor Museum. You can see the stone
throughout the walk, in boundary walls and buildings; it was much
used in the local area, e.g. for Birkenhead Town Hall, and was even
used in the construction of New York's Empire State Building. It has a
distinctive colour, much whiter than the red sandstone which you find
elsewhere on the Wirral.*

1. **Take the track signposted 'To Brimstage'.**

The hexagonal footpath sign where you start is one of several on
this walk. Some look fairly recently painted – probably done as part

of a local scheme, involving young offenders, to maintain these attractive landscape features.

There was a steeplechase course between Storeton and Barnston, one of several former racecourses on the Wirral (see also Walks 10, 14, 18, 19). A balcony on the rear of Lodge Farm (now a pets' boarding kennels) was used as a viewing point for the races.

2. **The track narrows to a path, at the end of which go through the kissing gate and straight ahead across a large field. By the motorway cross a stile and follow a path to reach a stile and the road. Turn left.**

3. **As the road bends left, take the signed path ahead to Higher Bebington. Follow over two more stiles. After a footbridge arc slightly anticlockwise, aiming uphill for a footpath sign to the right of the road ahead. Cross the sandstone stile and go left to the road.**

This is Red Hill Road. Some historians claim that a massive battle between Norsemen and Anglo-Saxons – the Battle of Brunanburh in the year AD937 – occurred on the Wirral, possibly on the ridge between Storeton and Higher Bebington. Folklore suggests that Red Hill was named after the blood that flowed down its slopes.

4. **A few metres uphill, take a signed footpath to the left, signed to Rest Hill Road (make sure you take the path to the left, rather than going down the driveway). Continue ahead when the path joins a track.**

Take a moment to glance slightly behind you to your left as you go along this stretch, taking in the fine views to the Clwydian hills of North Wales.

Just before you reach Rest Hill Road notice the flat path coming in from your right – the old line of Storeton Quarry tramway (see below).

5. **Go straight over at Rest Hill Road. You have an option here. The main route follows the clear path straight ahead. But the woodlands are beautiful, with some interesting things to see in**

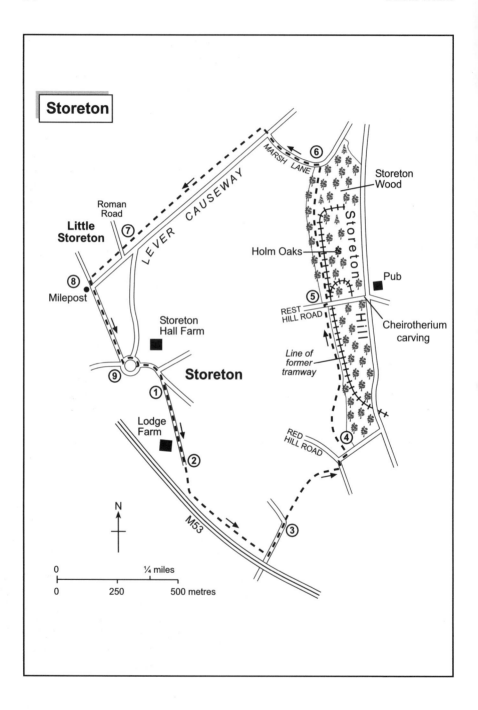

them, so you may like to bear immediately right and wander through the trees. If so, start with the cheirotherium carving (see below) and then wander, parallel with the road, to see the quarry outlines.

The main path is the track of a tramway, built in 1837 to take sandstone to a dock at Bromborough Pool. Horses pulled the tram trolleys along the horizontal sections of tram rail; gravity then let the trolleys roll down to Bromborough, with the speed controlled by a brakeman; the horses then pulled the empty trolleys back up the hill. The tramway went directly through the middle of the Lever Brothers factory site at Port Sunlight and was a source of annoyance to the Levers for years! You can see an example of the narrow tram rails 400m along the main path, next to an inscription.

The quarries (three in total) were higher up, near the main road, and were over 60 metres deep. They were mostly infilled in the 1930s by material excavated from the first Mersey road tunnel. You can still see some of their sunken outline today. Fossilised tracks of dinosaurs were found 20m down in 1838, and the animals were given a scientific name based on the quarry's location – *Cheirotherium storetonensis*. Examples of the tracks, also found on Hilbre Island, can be seen in Victoria Hall and Christchurch, b o t h in near by Higher Bebington (incidentally – if I may go off on an outrageous tangent – the Beatles played Victoria Hall in 1962!). In 2000 a life-sized carving of a cheirotherium was made on a quarried wall of sandstone, which you can find just off the path in the top right hand corner of the woods.

Amongst the wood's birdlife watch out for treecreepers, which climb spirally up tree-trunks, and nuthatches which, alone among British birds, walk down the trunks. There are also jays, lesser-spotted wood-peckers (listen for their loud drilling sound as they bore into the trees) and several types of butterfly. Three holm oaks,

The Storeton dinosaur carving

Pushchairs now trundle where a tramway once ran

planted at the edge of a clearing on your right after 200 metres, are evergreen trees with acorns that take two years to ripen.

6. **At Marsh Lane, turn left to reach the Lever Causeway. Cross the road and go left.**

This avenue was one of several created by Viscount Leverhulme, though most are on his private estate. They were part of his plan to build wide residential roads for the growing Wirral population and were to comprise a central road, with service roads each side. But with the coming of the First World War, the plan was never completed.

7. **As the road bends left, go straight ahead down Little Storeton Lane into the pretty hamlet of Little Storeton.**

'Roman Road' on your right wasn't named as such until 1938! It is certainly old, however – perhaps medieval and possibly linked to the Roman quarry work and the Roman road through Willaston (Walks 16 and 23).

8. **Turn left, following the road, by the National Cycle Network milepost.**

For more on the milepost, see page 149.

If you can see over the hedge to your left about 150 metres after the milepost you'll notice Storeton Hall Farm on the other side of the main road (if you are struggling to see it, go left at point 9 below, walking to just beyond the 'bends' road sign, but the trees may obscure your view when they are in leaf). You can glimpse a high wall, with a blocked up window, forming the gable end of a farm building. This is the most visible remaining section of a great hall, part of the original Storeton Hall built in the 1360s by the Stanley family. They were probably the most powerful Wirral family

Storeton Hall Farm: the wall of the Great Hall is on the left

in medieval times and there are many tales of them abusing their position at the expense of the long-suffering ordinary folk.

Their power came from holding the position of Chief Forester of Wirral. Wirral was a royal forest from about 1120 to the 1370s. This did not mean it was covered in trees, but that special protection was given to deer and other wild animals for hunting. Woe betide you if you stopped the deer getting food by protecting your crops with a fence, or if you failed to cut your dog's claws – they might hurt a boar. And if you were caught poaching, you would probably be blinded or killed. It was tough in those days!

Centuries later, the Stanleys were owners of Storeton Quarry.

9. **Just after the pretty 'Old School House', at the roundabout, take the second exit, Red Hill Road, back to the start.**

Walk 8: Eastham Country Park

**River views – outdoor sculptures – woodland –
a former pleasure gardens and zoo –
large ships (hopefully!) – Mersey ferry crossings**

Start and finish	Eastham Country Park car park, signposted from the A41, just north of Junction 5 of the M53
Distance	2¾ miles
Approximate time	1½-2 hours (the route can be shortened by ½ mile/750 metres by cutting out the loop at point 4)
Refreshments	Pubs and tea garden near the car park
Walking conditions	Fairly level; mostly good paths suitable for cycles and pushchairs (with many alternative paths available). This is one of those walks where (in the later stages) there are lots of criss-crossing paths. I've tried to describe an easy-to-follow route but don't worry if you take a wrong turn – you can never get seriously lost in the park

This walk combines great views up and down the Mersey, the variety and beauty of the woodlands at Eastham, some superb wood carvings and evidence of the area's varied history. A Visitor Centre, and a noticeboard opposite The Tap pub, give much interesting information. Eastham was an important crossing point between Liverpool and the Wirral for centuries. Its popularity waned when the railway opened between Birkenhead and Liverpool 1846, but the area was revived with the addition of the Eastham Ferry Hotel and Pleasure Gardens which included a zoo. These were a huge attraction for decades but declined in the 1920s. The last ferry – a paddle steamer – left in 1929.

1. **From the car park drop down the hill and turn right.**

   Opposite The Tap is a jetty, built in the 1870s to serve the Mersey ferry. The bay-fronted sandstone building nearby was the ticket office.

   Notice also the superb Marine Life sculptures nearby, celebrating the variety of sea creatures found around Wirral's coast. There are also decorative tiles made by local school children.

   600 metres to your right, just out of sight, is the entrance to the Manchester Ship Canal, The 35-mile canal linked Manchester with the sea for the benefit of traders, particularly cotton importers and textile exporters. It attracted millions of sightseers during its construction and was opened in 1894 by Queen Victoria. Today, if you are lucky with your timing, you can still see large ships heading to the canal carrying containers, coal, chemicals, oil and grain. If you enjoy New World wine from Tesco it may well have been shipped past here to the company's site at Irlam!

2. **Retrace your steps to the mini-roundabout, then walk along the riverside road/car park, which becomes a path.**

3. **Look for a gate in the metal fencing to your right.**

   This leads to Jobs Ferry, now just a collection of scattered sandstone blocks. This was the original site of the ferry station to cross the Mersey, which is believed to have operated since the 13th century, initially run by monks. Today, the green and red buoys in the river are used to guide ships using the canal.

4. **Continue on the main path to a fence of metal railings, marking the boundary of the park. For more, excellent views, continue ahead through a small car park and alongside the river for 350m keeping to the main path, next to green railings. (If you are not taking this extension, then turn left, up the unpaved path, just before the park's boundary railings.)**

   The raised grassy area to your left was once the site of the coal-fired Bromborough Power Station, now demolished. The large

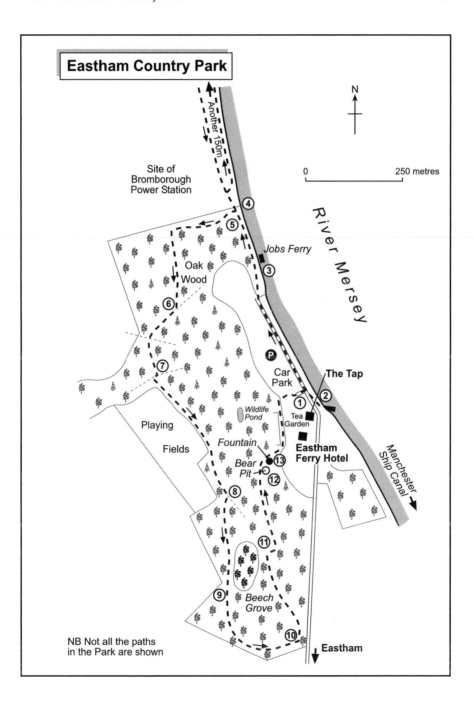

Job's Ferry: ships have been using the Mersey here for hundreds of years

concrete quay next to the river was the unloading area for ships bringing coal.

There are fine views of the Mersey. Liverpool is to the left, the airport to your half-right.

Return along the top of the grassy bank, which is accessible on your left shortly after the path bends away from the river.

Several rail lines to the power station once ran along this bank, part of an extensive rail network serving local industry, built from 1910 but now vanished. Today, when the gorse along here is in flower a scent of coconut fills the air.

5. **Turn right immediately after you get back to the park's metal fence, up an unpaved path. After 50 metres reach a grassy**

open area with benches. Keep to the right-hand side and take the first path right, downhill, to walk parallel with the metal fence.

The gentle hill you walk over is not natural. There used to be a sandstone quarry here, which was infilled with rubble from the demolition of the power station. The rubble was piled higher than the natural ground level, making an artificial hill.

After about 50 metres, where there is a gap in the (now wooden) fence to the right, turn left.

This path is lined with poplars to the left, though many came down in a storm a few years ago, their shallow roots unable to hold fast in the sandy soil. The sycamores to the right are thinned out from time to time as they crowd out other plants and damage the bank, which is retaining industrial waste.

6. **At a meeting of paths, by a sculpture called Oak Wood, fork right.**

There are concrete blocks each side of the path at the junction. These used to carry an overhead steam pipe from the power station.

After about 120 metres, where there is another concrete block to your right, and a wire fence corner immediately ahead, turn left. Keep to the main path to reach another junction.

Here you will find another sculpture – The Never-Ending Story – and the giant stump of a beech tree which children can climb inside. Beech and oak are the dominant trees in the woodland. This beech used to be the tallest tree on Wirral (at least 28 metres high) until 2003 when part of it came down in a storm and much of the rest had to be cut back. It is thought to be over 300 years old. The felled timber was used to make the marine life sculptures near the jetty.

7. **Turn right for a few metres, then take a path left, just before playing fields, and keep on it, ignoring paths to the left.**

You may notice bird-boxes along here and elsewhere in the wood. Some are for tawny and short-eared owls; others for tits. The boxes with no hole at the front are for bats, which enter through a slit underneath.

At a junction of paths, with a corner of the playing field to your right, continue straight ahead, signed to The Beech Grove.

Marine life carvings made from the ancient beech tree on the route

8. **120 metres later, fork right, down a clear path, signed with a white arrow (there is an oak tree in front of you at this fork). Keep to this path (but you may wish to detour right to the other side of a wall, when you see a sign, to see 'the Warrener's Seat' with its cute rabbits' heads and paws).**

Just under 250 metres after the fork you find Beech Grove to your left, by the 'Protecting the Future' sculpture. Beech Grove is a magnificent stand of mature beeches. It is also known as 'The Cathedral' – when the trees are in leaf the canopy forms a great cathedral-like ceiling, with scattered shafts of sunlight as if coming through the windows.

9. **Continue on the path, passing the wall on your right. Soon the path curves left.**

You pass several conifers with delicate, flat needles – these are Western hemlocks, often grown elsewhere for their timber or to make paper.

10. **Stay on the path as it bends left by a gate to the road, then 15 metres later, fork left up an unpaved path which winds through the woods.**

11. **Eventually, at a T-junction of paths, turn right. A few metres later turn left, and immediately afterwards keep to the right-hand fork in paths. Continue straight ahead, and soon fork to the right to go between low pillars at a break in a sandstone wall.**

The wall marks the edge of the old Pleasure Gardens. This area comprised magnificent gardens and many other attractions: a zoo with lions, leopards, camels, monkeys and more; entertainments including a ballroom, bandstand and stage; and fairground attractions including a water chute and loop-the-loop roller coaster, thought to be the first in the country. There are good pictures of the Gardens in the Visitor Centre.

Keep to the upper, left-hand, path and eventually reach green railings around the former zoo's circular Bear Pit (now containing carved bears).

12. **Continue in the same direction, along the main path and, down steps; soon reach one of four former sandstone fountains in the Gardens.**

Notice also a man-made 'cave' on the left – either for the water pump, or to house more animals.

13. **Pass the cave and continue downhill for 20 metres to a second fountain. Here turn left to join a main path, walking with the sloping wall of the former boating lake to your left. This takes you back to the start.**

Take a moment to look at the huge oak tree at the top of the children's play area next to the car park (one of its fallen branches has been carved into a dragon). This has been dated to at least 500 years old – before Henry VIII came to the throne.

Walk 9: New Brighton

**A former entertainment mega-resort – street art –
coastal walking – a lighthouse – a pretty park –
old and new sources of energy**

Start and finish	Atherton Street, New Brighton, at the Merseyrail station, 250 metres from the A554
Distance	Just under 3 miles
Approximate time	Allow at least two hours as there is so much to see
Refreshments	Two pubs at point 4; Vale House Café at Vale Park; numerous pubs and cafés in New Brighton
Walking conditions	Tarmac paths and pavements throughout (except one avoidable very short stretch of cobbles), suitable for pushchairs, cycles, etc

This is a route for a fine day, to catch the bracing sea air, great views and seaside atmosphere of New Brighton – you might even be able to have a donkey ride! Along the way you will find some excellent information boards about New Brighton in its heyday. There's also lots of street art to look out for.

The view you get from the station, downhill to the sea and across to Formby Point, would have been the first sight of New Brighton for millions of holidaymakers. The idea for the resort came from a Liverpool builder, James Atherton, who bought over 170 acres/70 hectares of sandy heathland to create a seaside resort fit for the cream of society – it would be the Brighton of the north. Over the following decades New Brighton became a hugely popular holiday and day-trip destination for people of all backgrounds.

Looking right from the station, at the very top of the hill you can see the huge copper-clad dome of Saints Peter and Paul Church built by a Catholic priest who wanted to match the great Basilica in Lisbon. It can hold 600 people but is currently closed, its future uncertain.

1. **Turn right from the station and then immediately left down Victoria Road. Continue in this direction, over traffic lights, to the seafront Promenade.**

The roadway after the traffic lights, with its wide tree-lined pavements and rows of bright awnings, gives a flavour of New Brighton a century ago.

2. **Turn right along the Tower Promenade.**

100 metres later, to the right of the turning circle, notice the carving of a tower on a block of sandstone; and about 30 metres further along the Prom there's a ring of brass figures set into the ground, wearing granite clothing – dancing to '50s '*rock*'?

To your right is Tower Grounds where New Brighton Tower once stood. This tower, finished in 1900 and standing 189 metres high, was like Blackpool's – but much bigger. The grounds covered 14 hectares and offered fantastic entertainment for visitors – a 3,000 seat theatre, a huge ballroom, a water flume to ride down, a fairground, restaurants, gardens and much more. The tower only lasted 19 years but the entertainment complex hosted top acts (including the Beatles) until 1969 when it burnt down.

New Brighton Tower and Lake
(*Reproduced by permission of Birkenhead Central Reference Library*)

Continue in the same direction, along Magazines Promenade taking in the views of Liverpool docks and the city.

Stop to admire the nine metal disks, called 'Spray', near the sandstone gateposts at the entrance to Vale Park. Children will enjoy working out the pictures on them; and can you find the elephant?! Next to 'Spray' stands an information plaque with an excellent guide to 'Birdlife in the Mersey Estuary'.

3. **Continue along the promenade, passing the war memorial, superbly carved in limestone, to the end of the grassy area on your right. Go up the cobbled lane, Pengwern Terrace, to The Magazine pub (known as 'The Mags') at the top and turn right along Magazine Brow.**

A magazine is a storage facility for ammunition and explosives and there was one in Magazine Lane in the 18th century. Ships unloaded their gunpowder on this side of the Mersey before being allowed to enter the Port of Liverpool – they could not risk a huge explosion in the docks. The pub dates from 1759 and there are several other quaint or unusual cottages and houses near it and The Pilot Boat pub (dated 1747) 75 metres further on.

The Magazine, named after an explosives storage facility in the 1700s

4. **Continue along the road, noting a sandstone turret and wall on your right.**

Soon, at the Magazine Lane road junction, there is a house with the most extraordinary front gate you will ever see! This used to be the entrance to Liscard Battery, built as a defence for the Mersey, but never used in anger. The turret you passed marked another corner but the Battery itself has long since disappeared.

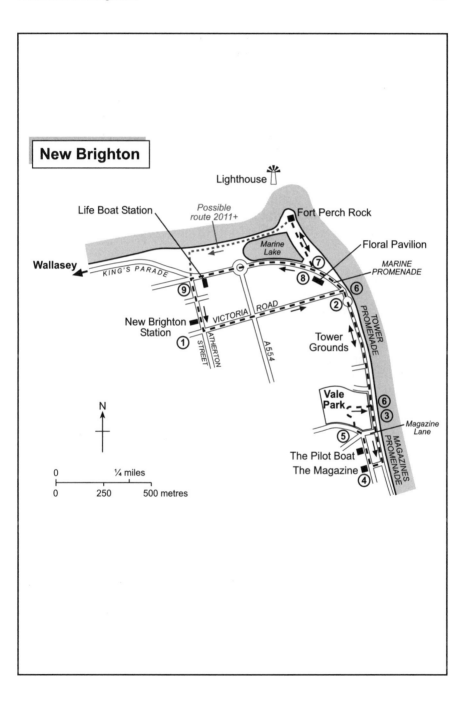

New Brighton

Lighthouse

Life Boat Station

Possible route 2011+

Fort Perch Rock

Floral Pavilion

Marine Lake

MARINE PROMENADE

Wallasey

KING'S PARADE

⑦

⑧

⑥

⑨

②

VICTORIA ROAD

TOWER PROMENADE

New Brighton Station

ATHERTON STREET

A554

①

Tower Grounds

Vale Park

⑥
③

Magazine Lane

N

⑤

MAGAZINES PROMENADE

The Pilot Boat

The Magazine

④

0	¼ miles
0	250	500 metres

5. **From the gateway fork left, up Magazine Lane, and a few metres later, turn right into Vale Park.**

Spend some time exploring the immaculately groomed park which was opened in 1899 by the local council who wanted to create more open space for a growing population. Amongst other things, the park has a café, which houses a small display about the local area, a rose garden and a bandstand. This is still used for brass bands, pop concerts and children's shows. Unusual trees in the park include evergreen holm oaks (there's one immediately left of the café), a fig tree and a mulberry. A friendly local resident told me how, when she was a child, she used to climb the mulberry to collect its leaves, the staple food of silkworms that she kept at school.

6. **Descend to the Prom and retrace your steps along it, maybe strolling along the sand if the tide is out (there are steps down, opposite the entrance to Vale Park).**

Stop just before the large red buoy, marked 'pier'. New Brighton Pier jutted out into the Mersey here until it was dismantled in 1978. As well as offering its own attractions the pier was the unloading point for ferries bringing crowds of visitors from Liverpool.

This corner section of the Promenade was once a narrow strip nicknamed 'Ham and Egg Terrace'. This was the rough end of town, full of cheap eating palaces and dodgy characters. Drunken behaviour and crime made it unsafe for many to use. The Terrace was pulled down in 1913 and replaced with the promenade you see today,

A statue commemorating the first guide dog for the blind

including the Floral Pavilion Theatre. Take a look at the carving of a dog – children will love it – by the theatre entrance. It marks the founding of the Guide Dogs for the Blind Association by Muriel Crooke in New Brighton in 1931.

7. **Back on the seaward side of the road (Marine Promenade) fork right into the entrance road for Fort Perch Rock car park (note two more sandstone carvings, one each side of the road entrance). Make your way to the left of the Fort to get a good view of New Brighton Lighthouse, maybe exploring the rock pools between the two buildings if the tide allows.**

Fort Perch Rock and the lighthouse were built on a sandstone outcrop that was a navigation hazard for shipping in and out of Liverpool. The rock was originally marked by a wooden structure or 'perch' but it was often washed away. It was replaced by the lighthouse, made of granite blocks, in 1830. Fort Perch Rock, meant

New Brighton lighthouse

as defence for Liverpool, was opened in the same year but never fired a shot in any battle. It did, however fire a warning shot across the bow of a ship that failed to identify itself in 1914 – the shot landed about 12km (7½ miles) away on Formby beach and was returned to the Fort! Today it houses a museum and exhibitions.

To your half-left, on a clear day, you can see the Liverpool Bay Douglas oil and gas complex in the far distance. Gas extracted from below the seabed is sent via a 34 km pipeline to a processing terminal at Point of Ayr, North Wales. Meanwhile, oil is piped 20 km from the drilling platform to a double-hulled supertanker permanently moored away from shipping lanes. Here the oil is transferred into tankers for international export.

The 25 wind turbines you can see are part of the 'Burbo Bank' windfarm, 7 km offshore. Its Danish owners claim that, if they were able to operate at maximum capacity, they would produce enough power for 80,000 homes (though in reality every wind farm operates at very substantially below maximum capacity because of the vagaries of our weather). Each turbine measures 137 metres from the base to the tip of the highest blade.

Important note: at the time of writing, New Brighton is undergoing extensive redevelopment work to create a major leisure and retail park. It is not currently possible to use the path from Fort Perch Rock west along the sea wall so the route below returns inland. Redevelopment work is due for completion in 2011 so, after then, you may prefer to use the sea wall path, diverting inland later to pick up the return route at point 9.

8. **Return to Marine Promenade and turn right to walk along the road. Continue past a roundabout with tropical trees on and then pass the lifeboat station. 20 metres later fork left, and stop at the junction at the bottom of the hill (Atherton Street).**

On the high ground to your left are several large houses with balconies. To your half-right is a sunken area of grass. It is extraordinary to realise that the grassy area – and, indeed the whole area of land to your right and ahead as far as you can see, is not 'solid ground' at all. The houses used to be perched on the tops of cliffs that dropped to a wide sandy beach – another one of New Brighton's great attractions. But there were serious problems with erosion by the sea, so in the 1930s a high sea wall was built. The huge expanse of land, which King's Parade runs along, was made by piling material that was being dug out of the new Mersey Tunnel on top of the old beach. Different coloured outcrops called 'Red Noses' and 'Yellow Noses', marking the tops of rocky prominences, are still visible a little further along the front, off our route, by Coastal Drive.

9. **Turn left up Atherton Street to return to the station.**

Walk 10: Raby

**A former racecourse – pretty woodland –
fine views – an ancient village**

Start and finish	By the Wheatsheaf Inn. Raby is along 'Upper Raby Road', off the A540 near Neston
Distance	About 3 miles
Approximate time	Allow 1½ hours
Refreshments	The Wheatsheaf Inn
Walking conditions	Easy walking; flat. May be a little muddy in places

This short, simple walk is a bit of a gem. Mostly following little-used paths and tracks, it often has a remote feel and offers a surprising variety of interest.

Please note that changes are planned by the farmer to the route between points 2 and 3 in late 2010. Before you start you may wish to check that either the route which is open as this book goes to publication – described below – is still available, or that signs at points 2 or 3 indicate that the

Sign to a place called 'By' in Sweden. Wirral villages such as Raby got their names from Scandinavian settlers

planned new route – also described below – is now open. The alternative is to walk along the road, which can be busy, for 550 metres/¹/₃ mile.

The starting point, Raby, is mentioned in the Domesday Book of 1086. The village name is Norse for 'village by a boundary' and may indicate that this is the southern limit of an area settled by Norsemen, after they had been driven out of Ireland in the 10th century AD. There are several other Wirral place-names ending in the Norse word 'by' (see photo).

The thatched and timber-beamed Wheatsheaf is known to date back to 1611 and may be much older. In 1997 the owner of the adjacent farm, who had developed an allergy to cows, took over the pub and the cowshed was converted into the restaurant!

1. **With your back to the pub, go right to Raby Road, then turn left into Raby Mere Road.**

Once, if you had turned right here, the road would have taken you to Raby Mere just over a mile away. The mere is an artificial lake, created as a pond to power a watermill in the early 17th century. Today, though, there is no direct road to the mill – the M53 has blocked it off.

A barn in Raby

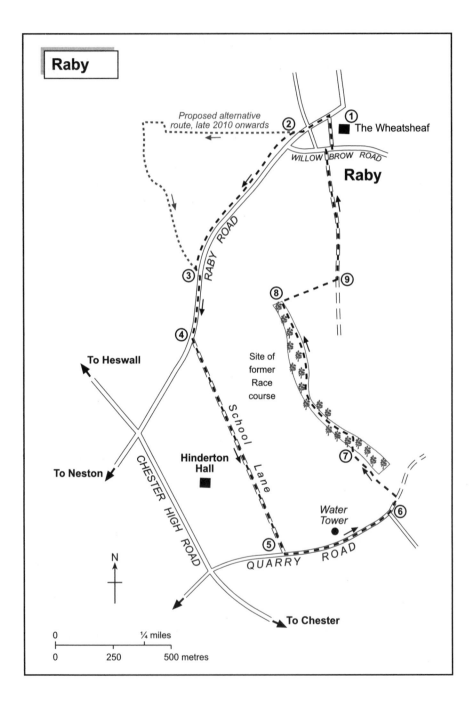

Raby

① The Wheatsheaf

Proposed alternative route, late 2010 onwards

② ③ ④ ⑤ ⑥ ⑦ ⑧ ⑨

WILLOW BROW ROAD

Raby

To Heswall

To Neston

Site of former Race course

RABY ROAD

School Lane

Hinderton Hall

Water Tower

CHESTER HIGH ROAD

QUARRY ROAD

N

To Chester

0   ¼ miles
0   250   500 metres

2. **20m after the telephone box go through the wooden gate to the right of the hedge adjacent to the road. The gate has a small 'MAFF Conservation Walks' label on it. Continue ahead, alongside the hedge.**

   Important note: in late 2010 the above 'permissive' path, which allows you to avoid walking along the road, is due to be closed. However the farmer advises that a new permissive route is being put in place. To take this route, from point 2 follow the clearly marked Footpath 49, alongside a hedge to your right. After a while this will meet the new permissive path where you turn left. Follow the new path to reach Raby Road and turn right along the verge at point 3. The approximate line of what I understand to be the new route is shown on the map.

   The spire of All Saints Church at Thornton Hough punctuates the fine views to the right.

3. **Keep on the path, running parallel to the road. When the path ends, continue along the verge.**

4. **Ignore a path signposted left down a tarmac driveway but, 25 metres later, cross the road and go down School Lane.**

   In the mid-19th century there was a viewing stand and horse racecourse to your left along School Lane, one of several race-courses on the Wirral (see also walks 7, 14, 18, 19). The lane's name comes from Neston's first school which was established at the Quarry Road end in 1610 – but no sign of it remains today.

   The track is lined with ash and sycamore trees. Many of the latter have been cut back to their base, as if they have been 'coppiced'. Under this ancient practice deciduous trees were cut right back to the stump. This encouraged new growth in the form of several shoots rising from the stump – called a 'coppice stool' – to make straight and sturdy poles. These might be used to make fences, or wattle for 'wattle and daub' walls in houses. Another benefit of coppicing is that it greatly prolongs the life of the tree. Many of the sycamores here have been allowed to grow into larger trunks.

Horses still use the quiet lane by the old racecourse

Just over halfway along the lane, to your right, you pass a sandstone house. This lodge was built in 1856 – one of three serving Hinderton Hall, visible beyond the lodge, built for Christopher Bushell, a philanthropist and Liverpool wine merchant. A later owner was Sir Percy Bates, chairman of the Cunard shipping company and friend of Rudyard Kipling who visited the hall.

Keep an eye open for large brown buzzards wheeling above the fields to your left.

5. **At the end of the lane, turn left into Quarry Road.**

After about 250m a glance over the fence of 'Theakston', on the right, reveals a quarry, one of three in Quarry Road. The sandstone here was used in road building. There was another quarry on the opposite side of the road. This yielded good building stone, which was used for the large, round water tower you can glimpse from the road behind Tower Cottage. The tower, built in 1884, has been skilfully converted into a house built on four levels.

Continue, on the right-hand side, to where the road bends sharp right, crossing very carefully beforehand.

This is true: just round the corner, on the right, once stood a place called 'Sod Hall'. There's nothing there today either!

6. **At the bend, go straight ahead into Bluebell Lane. Before reaching 'Rose House' go through a metal kissing gate tucked in the hedge on your left. Follow the right-hand field boundary, passing more old quarries to the right.**

7. **At the corner of the field go through a gap in the hedge a few metres after a stile (this saves your legs!) to enter Cherry Wood. Go left, keeping to the main path.**

Cherry Wood is a stretch of delightful deciduous woodland. It marks an ancient boundary between Neston and Raby and analysis of the plant life suggests it has been wooded for centuries.

When the views open up you can see the Liverpool skyline and, on a good day, 30 miles away to the north-east, Winter Hill topped by its giant TV mast. The top of the mast is 750 metres above sea level. Much nearer, Willaston Mill can be seen poking above the trees to the right.

8. **At the T-junction of paths, by stone gateposts, turn right.**

9. **Cross the stile to the farm track and go left, keeping on the track to reach the walk's start point (you may have to go through or over gates shut by the farmer).**

A question for children: what is odd about the upstairs window of the cottage just before you reach Willowbrow Road?

Walk 11: Thurstaston Common and Royden Park

Great views – a miniature railway – woodland and meadow – a sacrificial stone (or not!) – heathland – Hillbark House

Start and finish	Thurstaston Common car park on the A540, 250m from the Cottage Loaf pub; (or at Royden Park, starting the walk at point 5)
Distance	3 miles
Approximate time	Allow 2 hours
Refreshments	Cottage Loaf pub near Thurstaston car park; Farmer's Arms near entrance to Royden Park; teashop may be open at weekends at Royden. Numerous picnic spots
Walking conditions	Mostly easy, dry walking; some uneven ground over rocks near the start

I always thought that Thurstaston Common was a very popular spot for a stroll. But when I've walked this route – often in perfect walking weather – I've been surprised to go for long stretches without seeing another person, so maybe this lovely walk will be new to you.

It covers the 'Royden Park and Thurstaston Local Nature Reserve'. Royden is an area of open spaces, meres (lakes) and coniferous and deciduous woodland, much of which has developed from old plantations. Thurstaston is a mix of heathland – characterised by heathers, gorse and birch – and woodland, most of which has established itself naturally.

1. **From the car park go through the wide gap in the logs by a notice board and climb the sandy path. Continue uphill to the viewpoint.**

   There are great views from here – to North Wales (including Anglesey on a clear day); up the Lancashire coast; and across to Liverpool and the Pennines in the distance. You can see three wind farms, which take advantage of the winds sweeping from the west: to your right, off the Lancashire coast, is Burbo Bank with 25 turbines; off the tip of the Welsh coast, near Prestatyn, is the North Hoyle array (30 turbines) and, further along the Welsh coast, is Rhyl Flats (25 turbines; you need reasonably clear weather to see that far).

   Around you is the heathland area of Thurstaston Common. Heathland is characterised by poor soils, which only a limited range of plants including heathers, gorse and bilberry can tolerate. Birch, oak and red-berried rowan also try to get a foothold in the soil. Heathland habitat is under threat across the UK and, as Thurstaston is the largest and best remaining example in Merseyside, it has been designated as a Site of Special Scientific Interest (SSSI).

   The flat-topped concrete structure you passed near the top of the hill is a triangulation pillar (often called a 'trig point'), made as part of a process started in the 1930s to accurately map the whole of the UK. 6173 were built and the job was not finished until 1962. My guess is that this is the most visited trig point on the Wirral.

2. **Drop a few metres back to the main path and go left, keeping to this path along the ridge. It gently descends, but you should continue to have good views for some time; do not drop onto the lower ground to your left.**

   Eventually you enter oak and birch woodland – just continue along the main path. Avoid any paths branching to left or right and eventually reach a wall in front of you.

   It is hard to imagine now but the Royden Park area was largely fields until the mid-19th century. The walls formed part of the field boundaries.

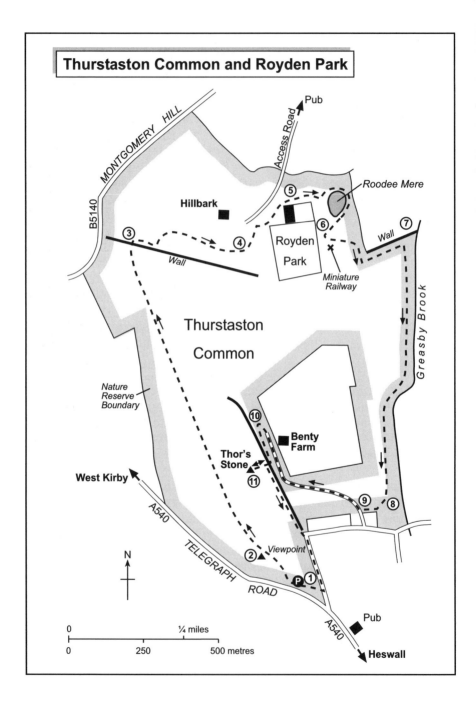

Thurstaston Common and Royden Park

MONTGOMERY HILL

B5140

Access Road

Pub

Hillbark

⑤

Roodee Mere

⑥

Royden
Park

⑦

Wall

③ ······→ ④

Wall

Miniature
Railway

Greasby Brook

Thurstaston

Common

Nature
Reserve
Boundary

⑩

Benty
Farm

Thor's
Stone

⑪

West Kirby

A540

⑨ ⑧

TELEGRAPH

N

② Viewpoint

ROAD

Ⓟ ①

A540

Pub

Heswall

0   ¼ miles

0   250   500 metres

The paths around the common can be surprisingly empty

3. **Go through the gap in the wall and turn right. After about 100 metres, as the path splits at pine trees, turn left. Soon reach an open area and turn right, following the main path up the meadow.**

Soon Hillbark, a mock-Tudor mansion, comes into view on the left. Extraordinarily, this great house used to sit on Bidston Hill and was moved brick by brick in 1931 to its current position by Sir Ernest Royden, after whom the park is named. It is now run as a hotel but retains extraordinary internal architectural features including a fireplace created by influential 18th century designer Robert Adam; stained-glass windows by the Pre-Raphaelite William Morris (whose designs are still popular in fashion and interior decorating today) and another fireplace once owned by Sir Walter Raleigh.

In summer the meadow is full of flowers, including birdsfoot trefoil with its curved yellow petals; and common spotted orchid with pink flowers and leaves marked with dark spots. The meadow attracts many butterflies.

4. **At the top of the meadow, fork left of the metal bench and go up a short hill, alongside a wooden fence. At the top of the hill fork left and take a clear path across a small open area and between rhododendron bushes.**

    At some brown metal posts (without a gate) turn right to the car park. Make your way through the car park, bearing slightly left to reach buildings.

5. **Walk to the left of the buildings and high wall, past a green metal gate, signed to 'Roodee Mere'.**

    Stop off at the Walled Nature Garden, managed through the Royden Park Project, a horticulture and woodwork employment training

Turning the miniature steam train at the end of the line

project for adults with learning difficulties, run by Wirral Social Services. There is much to look at including a wildlife pond, herb garden and several sculptures.

Continue down the track to bend right and cross the miniature railway line. Go clockwise round Roodee Mere.

The railway is usually open on summer Sunday afternoons and on Bank Holiday Mondays. Admire the working scale model engines – or join the nearby queue to ride one!

6. **After going round the mere you reach fenced off areas of railways sidings. Go left here, taking the signed path to Irby Hill and Thurstaston Wood. Follow the main path, which bends right after 100 metres or so. 50 metres later look for a stone wall starting on your left. Turn left and walk with the wall on your left for about 200 metres.**

7. **At the bottom of the hill do not cross the footbridge, but go right and follow the path beside Greasby Brook for almost 500 metres through woodland filled with the sweet scent of Scots pine and the sound of bird song.**

Some of the tree trunks along here are bright orange, covered with an alga called *trentepohlia* which likes darkish, damp locations in western Britain.

At a cross-paths, go straight ahead, taking the narrow path immediately left of a large wooden bench. Soon the path turns right and widens, and you eventually start to walk with a wire fence to your right.

8. **Continue to the corner of the fence (ignoring a gate shortly before the corner). At the corner, fork right along a clear path.**

When you reach another path, by a field corner, turn right and immediately go through a gateway. Continue, to meet a track.

9. **Go straight ahead, along the track, for about 400 metres to pass pretty Benty Farm.**

There are several 'Benty' names on the Wirral. They probably come from 'Bent hay', bent being a kind of hay grass. Bent is also a medieval word for an unenclosed pasture or heath.

10. **Shortly after the farm, the track narrows – a few metres later double back to your left, down a path which carries you over marshy ground. Go though a gate in the wall and straight ahead for 50 metres to reach Thor's Stone.**

There are many theories about the origins of this huge rock with its extraordinary curved gullies – most dramatically that it was a place of worship and sacrifice for Viking settlers. The truth is probably more mundane: it is more likely to have been the mount for a crane in an old sandstone quarry.

11. **Retrace your steps and turn right immediately before the wall. Continue ahead to reach the road and go straight on, along a track. About 50 metres after the end of the school buildings look for any of the paths through trees to your right, back to the car park.**

Walk 12: Brimstage and Thornton Hough

Craft centre – wildlife – an environmentally friendly farm estate – historic villages

Start and finish	Brimstage Hall Courtyard, 1 mile from the Clatterbridge roundabout on the A5137 (M53 junction 4)
Distance	3¼ miles
Approximate time	Allow 1¾ hours, plus stopping time at Brimstage and Thornton Hough
Refreshments	The Seven Stars pub in Thornton Hough; tea and coffee shops in both villages
Walking conditions	Level ground throughout, generally good paths, but parts can be a little muddy when wet

Most of this walk is across attractive land which is managed as an environmentally friendly farm. It also takes in the attractive villages of Brimstage and Thornton Hough, each with very different histories. Start with a look around the Brimstage Hall development: the craft shops are great places for gift ideas. Also here is Brimstage Farm Park, with its popular annual 'Maize Maze' and other attractions, and a Countryside Education Centre planned at the time of writing.

1. **Go through the gateway with sandstone pillars each side at the lower corner of the courtyard and cross the parking area.**

From here you can see the top of the three-storey tower at the back of Brimstage Hall. It's probably 700-800 years old and may have been a pele tower – a rectangular, fortified residence more usually found in the Scottish borders. The tower has 'machicolations' – overhanging holes at the top from which things could be dropped

Brimstage Hall

on attackers – and arrow slits. The Hall also once had a moat – though in medieval times moats were more often status symbols than needed for defence.

Go down the driveway and along the road for about 150 metres.

Large village greens are unusual in Cheshire (historically, this is Cheshire) – Brimstage's was created in 1913. On the far side is a white barn bearing a datestone of 1758.

2. **Take the footpath signposted right to Thornton Hough, using sandstone steps. Follow this path straight head and cross a farm track, via two stiles.**

The field immediately after the sandstone steps is very bumpy – I've always wondered why. Maybe there were houses here centuries ago, or perhaps part of it has been quarried and then filled in with

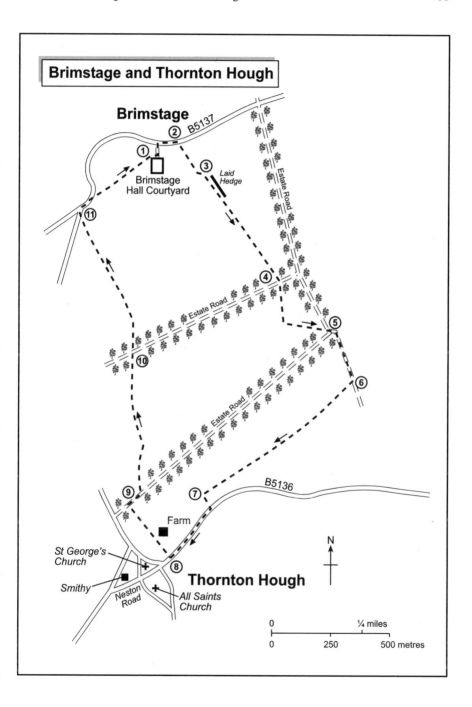

Brimstage and Thornton Hough

Brimstage

B5137

② B5137

① Brimstage Hall Courtyard

③

Laid Hedge

Estate Road

④

⑤

⑥

⑩ Estate Road

⑪

Estate Road

B5136

⑨

Farm

⑦

St George's Church

Smithy

Neston Road

⑧ **Thornton Hough**

All Saints Church

N

0 ¼ miles

0 250 500 metres

rubble – Brimstage sits on sandstone which is just below the surface; this stone would have been easily accessible for building walls and buildings.

3. **Bear slightly left, then over another stile and walk to the right of a hedge.**

The hawthorn hedge is 'laid' from time to time. The stems are virtually cut through and then, as you can see, bent almost ninety degrees to near-horizontal. This encourages strong new growth, thickening the hedge and prolonging its life, as well as making a more attractive habitat for wildlife.

Near the far-right-hand corner of the field, you can see a box on top of a pole. This is for barn owls to nest in.

At a field junction the path moves to the left of a hedge, but keeps in the same direction.

Hedge laying alongside this field

Keep your eyes open for a variety of wildlife including buzzards wheeling, kestrels hovering, pheasants and partridges. I have seen several brown hares at close-quarters along this stretch.

4. **Cross a tree-lined track and go straight cross a field to reach a T-junction of paths. Turn left along a sunken path to meet a firm estate track opposite a clump of conifers.**

This impressive avenue, and others including the well-known Lever Causeway at Storeton, were built by the first Viscount Leverhulme (who also built the attractive estates in Port Sunlight and Thornton Hough). He planned to put residential housing along them, and allowed space for a central road and an outer service road on each side. But with the outbreak of the First World War, his plan was never fulfilled.

5. **The tracks to left and right are private so go straight over the junction, passing left of the conifers, onto a track that soon bends right (ignore the track that forks to the left on the bend).**

Along here, the view left reveals Liverpool Anglican Cathedral in the distance, dominating the skyline.

6. **After about 220 metres pass a metal gate and 20 metres later, at another metal gate, turn right over a stile, to walk alongside a hedge. Meet and follow a line of telegraph poles and stay on this heading to reach a track.**

7. **Turn left to meet the B5136. Cross to the pavement and turn right to walk into Thornton Hough. If you wish, wander down the main road through the village.**

Thornton Hough is an ancient settlement, mentioned in the 1086 Domesday Book. However the village we see today is the product of two successful businessmen – The Victorian Joseph Hirst, a Yorkshire woollen manufacturer and William Lever (later Viscount Leverhulme) who established the successful soap factory at Port Sunlight in 1888.

Hirst built several buildings at the upper end of the village – you can see his initials on The Turret. But Lever was responsible for the rest, most of which were to house his estate workers.

The village has two large churches – the Parish church with the tall spire built by Hirst, and St George's Church, with its squat tower, by Lever. (Lever did not want the church to dominate the village so, as well as having a low tower, he lowered the ground the church was on by over a metre). From the top of the village, you will notice the Parish church has five clocks – Hirst added the extra one, as the roof of the church did not allow him to see the clock from his bedroom window.

Look at the weather vane on Lever's church – a cockerel and bugle. This is a visual pun on his name: 'lever' in French means 'to get up', and the cock and the bugle are both forms of early morning wake-up calls!

There is an extraordinary mix of architecture here: sometimes you can see black and white carved timbers, elsewhere brick or sandstone block. Roofs are made from thatch, slate and coloured tile, and even the chimneystacks are elaborate. Take a look at the first few houses on Neston Road to see ornately carved woodwork (above the windows and on the gable of no. 1); pargetting (decorative plasterwork, on no. 2 above the windows); stone carving, and ornamental ironwork on doors and windows (on nos. 3 and 4). It's also worth looking at the picturesque smithy at the bottom of the hill, especially if it's operating (sadly, though, its thatched roof was recently removed).

8. **After looking around, retrace your steps and take the track with a barrier at the entrance, signed 'Public Footpath to Brimstage', near the red telephone box.**

You will pass farm buildings on your right. The farm, tenanted from the Leverhulme Estate, is managed under the Countryside Stewardship Scheme, in an environmentally friendly way. Wildlife is encouraged, for example by providing the boxes for barn owls as well as ones for tree sparrows. New hedges, trees and areas of wildflowers are planted, which also provide wildlife havens; animals are reared humanely; and the use of chemicals is extremely carefully controlled.

9. After 250m, reach an estate road. Turn right for 40 metres, then left down a clear path signed to Brimstage. Continue on this path crossing two stiles – each incorporating a slab of sandstone. From the second you get a good view of Thornton Manor gatehouse to your half-left. Continue on the clear path, passing a small stand of Scots pine with their characteristic bare lower trunks.

Thornton Manor was built by Lever and is a beautiful building with elaborate internal decoration and landscaped gardens. The third Lord Leverhulme entertained many members of royalty here including the Queen Mother, Prince Philip and Princess Margaret. Today it is an exclusive venue for weddings and conferences.

10. Cross another estate road, lined with sycamores, via two kissing gates. Then bear slightly right to reach another sandstone slab stile. Cross and continue ahead, to reach a further stile and, a few metres later, a path junction. Continue straight ahead. After 500 metres you will come to a road.

On your right, you will see a large area of deciduous trees, planted in 2004 as part of the farm's land stewardship scheme.

11. Turn right for 150m. When the road bends left, take the footpath by the black and white traffic chevrons to take you back to Brimstage Hall.

Walk 13: Frankby and Larton

Parkland and farmland – giraffe food – a former
RAF camp – a tree plantation – old farming
methods – traditional buildings

Start and finish	Royden Park car park, off the B5140 which runs between Caldy and Frankby
Distance	3½ or 3¾ miles
Approximate time	Allow 2 hours
Refreshments	Picnic sites, and teashop occasionally open, at Royden Park; Farmer's Arms pub at Frankby
Walking conditions	Flat with some gentle slopes; often good tracks and paths, but the sections across fields can be very muddy, especially in winter

This is a varied walk through woodland, farmland and an unusual plantation. Many of the paths are little used so the route often feels remote despite being near built-up areas. There are magnificent old buildings around point 6 and at Frankby, worth taking time to admire.

Royden Park was farmland until the mid 19th century. Now, attractions include a walled nature garden, and model railways offering rides on Sundays and bank holidays, subject to the weather.

1. **At the four-way crossing just before the car park, take the track signed to Frankby Mere and Montgomery Hill.**

2. **Go past a metal gate, and 125 metres later, opposite a gate on the right, take a signposted path to the left to make a clockwise circuit of Frankby Mere.**

The circuit of this man-made pond, which is becoming increasingly dry even in winter, provides a pleasant detour through Corsican and Scots pine, birch and the occasional oak. I love the tunnel of rhododendrons, with their long, twisting branches, towards the end of the circuit.

I suggest you take the clear path left, about 100 metres after the start of the circuit and follow it as it forks right into an open area that is ideal for picnics. On the far side is a red-barked 'Madrona' tree, a native of North America, and said to be the best example in Britain. To its right is a fine Deodar Cedar, from Asia.

Giraffes at Chester Zoo, happy consumers of foliage from Royden Park (*Photo: Chester Zoo*)

You will notice that some of the trees in the mere have been severely cut back. These are willows, which are coppiced every four years (for more on 'coppicing' see page 77) by the team at the Royden Park Project, which provides employment training for adults with learning difficulties. The cut branches are sent to feed the giraffes at Chester Zoo.

3. **Back on the track, continue to a road. Cross and go right for 100m. Turn left between walls, by the 'Birch Heys, Private Road' sign, and immediately right, signed to Grange.**

Notice how the fields to your left are long and quite narrow. They grew out of the 'old ridge and furrow' farming system used in the middle ages. Land for farming was not split into fields surrounded by the hedges we take for granted in the countryside today. Instead land was divided into long thin strips which were banked up to form 'ridges' a few metres wide, with shallow ditches – 'furrows' – in between. The whole of the arable land would be divided into these strips, large groups of which formed 'open fields'. The strips were allocated to the people who lived in the village to grow their crops on. This allocation was often apparently haphazard so that someone might own one strip in one place and another one 100 metres away – it was a very inefficient way of farming. Later the pattern of the long strips was used as the basis for laying out the fields we see today.

4. **Go straight over the road and down 'Frankby Stiles' towards the riding complex and kennels at Larton, passing landscaped fishing ponds. Later, do not take the turning for the farm, but continue straight ahead along the tarmac track which becomes unmade. At the end turn left and soon cross a concrete bridge and stile.**

5. **Follow the field boundary on your left to reach a stile. Cross it and aim diagonally right, to the field corner, just left of a house.**

You are walking over a series of ridges about 15m wide. These, again, are the remains of the 'ridge and furrow' farming system. One advantage of this system is that the furrows improved drainage of the sticky clay soil.

6. **Cross the stile and turn right, later following the road round the corner to the right.**

The house by the stile, China Plate Farm, is named after the plate you can see set into the farmhouse wall. The farm was built in the 1700s by a former Mayor of Liverpool. Just after the farmhouse, notice the large entrance to the long brick barn, and a similar doorway on the far side. These used to help farmers with 'winnowing' – separating the grain they had harvested from its husk, the chaff. When the two parts were separated inside the barn, the draft through the doors (which face the prevailing wind) blew the lighter chaff away. The triangular sections sticking out from each side of the entrance supported the open doors, which funnelled the wind through the barn.

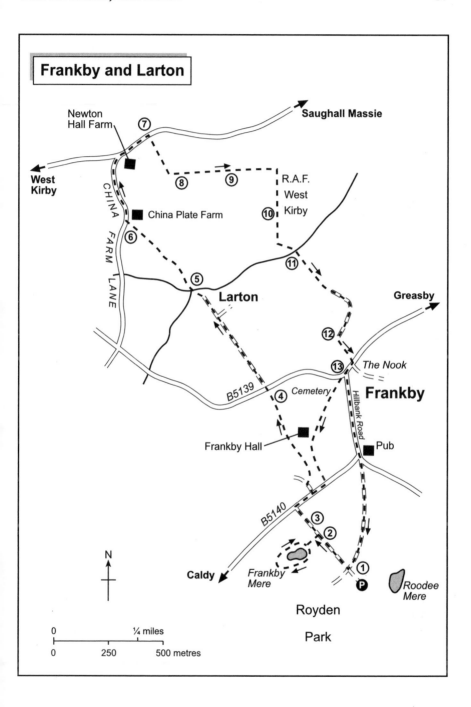

7. **Soon after Newton Hall Farm, opposite a modern bungalow (Newton Hall Cottage), cross the stile; over a track and continue over two more stiles. With the pond on your left, follow the hedge to a fourth stile.**

8. **From the stile, continue on the same heading, towards the left-hand side of trees visible over the brow of the hill, across the field.**

To your left you can see the 25 wind turbines of the 'Burbo Bank' windfarm, 7 km offshore. Its Danish owners claim that they can produce enough power for 80,000 homes. Each turbine measures 137 metres from the base to the tip of the highest blade (for more info. see www.burbo.info).

9. **Cross a stile next to the woodland and continue ahead to reach a track. Turn right, to take the track through the plantation.**

The tracks are part of the site of former RAF West Kirby, the buildings and roads of which were laid out in a grid system. No

RAF West Kirby in 1947 (Photo credit – see Preface)

aircraft were ever based here; instead, it was used as a WWII transit camp for British airmen waiting to go overseas, and airmen from allied countries who came here to fight. After the war, it became a 'boot camp' for men doing National Service.

10. **Keeping in the same direction go through two gates and under power lines after which the track narrows. When it forks, bear left down a narrow path to cross a wooden footbridge.**

11. **Walk up the field, with the field boundary to your left, to reach a stile, after which take the track ahead.**

12. **Immediately before the stables, take the footpath to the right signed 'To Frankby' (there are further obvious 'ridges' in the field to your right). Turn right when you reach the road and cross to the small village green.**

Frankby and West Kirby both have 'by' name endings, indicating they were settled by Norsemen who came to the Wirral just after AD900 (see photo, page 74). Similarly, the first part of the name 'Larton' comes from 'leirr', an Old Norse word for clay – your muddy boots will tell you this is an apt name!

There are many lovely old buildings clustered around and near Frankby's green. This is a Conservation Area and the buildings are mostly made of traditional materials: sandstone, hand-made brick and slate roofs. Many have datestones from the 1700s, and Half Inn House, up 'The Nook' (leading off the green), says '1675'.

13. **At the junction, you have a choice. Either:**

a) Go left, up Hillbark Road, for a slightly shorter route and to pass the pub; continue up the road to the entrance to the park. Cross and continue up the access road; or

b) To take in the peace of Frankby Cemetery, and to admire Sir Thomas Royden's castle-like house, cross the road and enter the cemetery between the stone gateposts. Continue ahead, eventually going clockwise round the house.

Frankby Hall with its castle-like features

The cemetery land used to be owned by Royden, the grandfather of Ernest whom the park is named after. Sir Thomas was a shipbuilding millionaire, and the cemetery's chapel and administration HQ were once his grand home, Frankby Hall. He built it in 1847 in the fashionable 19th century style – like a castle, with turrets, crenellations (battlements), solid buttresses (thick, vertical wall supports) and even mock arrow-slits.

Take the path left immediately after the building to reach the road. Turn right and retrace your steps to the start.

Walk 14: Parkgate

A former major seaport, fishing village and seaside resort – disused railways – coastal walking – saltmarsh – wildlife – great views

Parkgate in 1915. The Donkey Stand is on the right – compare
the height of the wall today

The open views of Parkgate are refreshing at any time. But the area can be particularly spectacular during the highest tides when water laps the Parade. The marsh is part of the Gayton Sands reserve owned by the Royal Society for the Protection of Birds. At high tides, the mass of birds in flight is particularly noisy and spectacular, including short-eared owls, merlins and sparrowhawks. Call Wirral Country Park Visitor Centre (0151-648-4371) for tide times and natural history information.

Though it is hard to imagine now, Parkgate was once a major port. Where you see the marsh, many-masted sailing ships once floated, often travelling between here and Ireland. The River Dee originally ran all the way along this side of the estuary from Chester but, due to silting,

Start and finish	At the 'Donkey Stand' (the small area that juts out slightly into the marshland, near The Ship hotel) on The Parade. Parkgate is signposted from the A540. (If parking is tricky on The Parade then start the walk at point 2 where there is a good parking area)
Distance	3½ or 5¼ miles
Approximate time	Allow 2 or 3 hours
Refreshments	A café and several pubs in Parkgate. Points 2 and 11 are good picnic spots
Walking conditions	Mostly flat; two climbs (one very short; the other a little longer but gentle). The odd muddy stretch/patch is possible, especially just after point 5 and between points 11 and 12 but these can be avoided by taking short cuts

was diverted via the Welsh side in 1737 for some of its length. However, the silting continued and the river eventually became too shallow for large ships to moor locally – the last one left in the 1820s.

1. **Walk along The Parade past the Boathouse pub, reaching a car park at The Old Baths.**

As you wander along the Parade keep an eye open for tall grey herons standing on, or flying over, the marsh; you may also see little egrets – smaller, upstanding bright white birds that were very rare in this country until recently, but are now found in several colonies around Britain including at Parkgate.

About 400 metres/¼ mile from the start, where the road temporarily narrows, you will see a sloping slipway down to the marsh (one of three along The Parade). Fishing was an important industry here, especially when Parkgate was no longer a major seaport. Fishing boats moored right against the slipways to bring

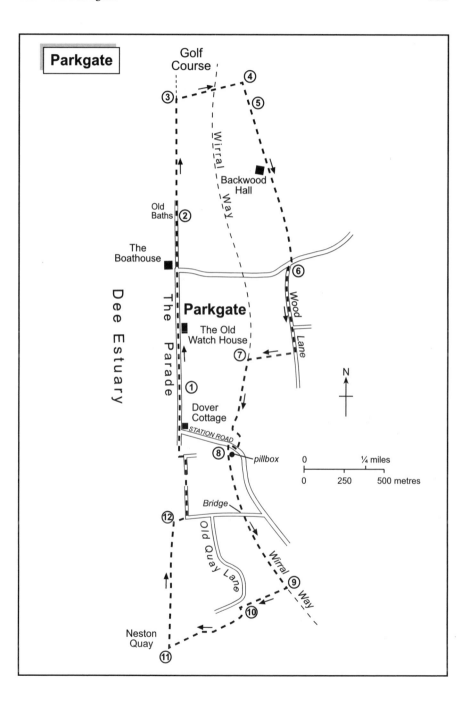

their catches ashore – the shore was several feet lower than today (see photo). There is another slipway just before the Boathouse pub.

The house where the road narrows, The Old Watch House, is where Customs Officers once lived who monitored Parkgate's international trade.

The area to your left at the car park, where a few grey walls still stand, is the remains of a large seawater swimming pool – The Old Baths – opened in the 1920s. The owner once wrote a fake complaint letter to a newspaper about the 'indecent' swimsuits on show. This pulled in more custom!

As well as being a port, shipbuilding also went on in Parkgate throughout the 1700s. Many shipbuilders are recorded locally (as well as related trades such as anchorsmiths and ropemakers) and one of the shipyards is believed to have been in this area of the village, though the exact location is unknown. Several of the ships went on to be used in the slave trade.

2. **At the end of the car park continue ahead, to follow the sea wall for 500 metres. At a sandstone pillar and wooden bench take the signed path right.**

3. **Cross the golf course with care, between the blue poles. Go over the Wirral Way and continue to the top of the hill (If you want to avoid a possibly muddy stretch turn right along the Wirral Way and rejoin at point 7). At the top take in the magnificent views while you get your breath back!**

4. **Go up some stone steps and turn right through trees. Follow the obvious path, which rejoins the golf course, to a gate.**

5. **Continue in the same direction across a field, down a dip, through gates and up the short hill. Continue ahead, along the track passing Backwood Hall, built in the Victorian Gothic architectural style, including a bell tower.**

6. **Cross into Wood Lane. After 600 metres take a path on the right, signposted to Parkgate.**

Parkgate saltmarsh and village

Parkgate is named after a deer park established about 750 years ago. The path you are on is thought to be the northern boundary of the park.

The large field to your left as you come down the path – Parksfield – was a popular venue for horse racing in the 19th century.

7. **Veer right just before the bridge, then go left and cross it. Continue on the Wirral Way to Station Road.**

The Wirral Way is a disused railway track. When the line was first opened in 1866 Parkgate Station was situated on the far side of Station Road. From there, you could catch the train to Hooton, linking with the main Birkenhead to Chester railway line. The line was popular with Victorian day-trippers who could reach the seaside easily; it also gave easy access to more distant markets for Parkgate's fishermen. In 1886, the railway line was extended to

West Kirby and the station moved to the other side of the road, where you have just walked. The south side became sidings, and handled the wagons coming to and from Ness Colliery (Walk 24).

8. **For the short cut, turn right down to The Parade (see the note after point 12 below). For the longer walk, cross the road at the bend and turn right. After 50 metres go left through the kissing gate and up the steps to a World War II 'pillbox' lookout point. Continue straight ahead, across the parking area, to a gate on the far side. Continue ahead, along the Wirral Way.**

Later, walk under a bridge, still stained with soot from the steam trains. About 125 metres after the bridge, where the good path swings left, a small embankment with trees on top forks off to the right. This was the line of a branch railway that ran down to Ness Colliery at Little Neston. (Don't take this fork, though; keep to the Wirral Way)

9. **Ignore crossing paths by a wooden waymarking post but continue to second post, where there is a gate to your left and then a white, shuttered, slate-roofed house. Turn right here, through a wooden kissing gate. Follow the path down the field, with the hedge on your right.**

At the bottom of the field, by a telegraph pole, the route is crossed by parallel hedges. Again, this is the line of the old railway to the colliery. Continue ahead, to reach a metal kissing gate.

10. **At the gate, turn left and follow the clear gravel path across a field. At the end of the field cross a footbridge and continue, keeping the hedge to your left, through another kissing gate, eventually reaching the edge of the marsh.**

This point is the Old Quay (also called Neston Quay). Now dismantled, the quay was a stone structure jutting into the Dee which, at that time, ran alongside the Wirral shore. It was built in the 16th century as a mooring place for ships trading with Chester, which had silted up. You can still see the brick remains of a building built to serve the shipping, in the area overgrown by trees on your left, just before you reach the marsh. Amongst other things this building was an inn and a 'house of correction' for vagrants. It was blown up by allied forces during World War II.

11. **Turn right, over a footbridge, to follow the obvious path over three more bridges, eventually going through a kissing gate. Continue along the marsh edge.**

Just after the gate you will probably pass reed mace (or bulrushes) on your left with their female flower heads looking like brown sausages. Soon after, you pass huge stands of common reed, which shimmer in the light and rustle in the breeze. The tough stems of reeds like this make them valuable for thatching roofs.

12. **After 700m, just before bungalows, the path detours inland along a road, then a footpath between wooden fences, and back along a road. 200 metres after the end of the footpath section, at a right-hand bend, take the narrow path on your left to take you back to The Parade (passing another slipway).**

Parkgate had several famous visitors. In 1784, Emma Hamilton, who was born at nearby Ness and who became the mistress of Admiral Lord Nelson, came here to treat a skin complaint by bathing in the waters. Parkgate had been a popular sea-bathing resort since the 1700s, when the golden sands were several feet below the present marsh. Emma stayed at Dover Cottage, the last terraced cottage before the bend at the south end of the Parade (next to it is Nelson Cottage, named after a boy who lived there who drowned in the Mersey). Other visitors to Parkgate included the composer, Handel, who travelled here from Ireland, and John Wesley, the founder of Methodism, who preached nearby.

Finally, at the end of a good walk, it's time to treat yourself to a famous Parkgate ice cream!

Walk 15: Thurstaston and Wirral Country Park

A waterfall – beach walking – wildlife – the Wirral Way – Ice Age cliffs – a rail accident

Start and finish	Wirral Country Park Visitor Centre at Thurstaston, signposted off the A540 between Heswall and West Kirby
Distance	3¾ miles
Approximate time	Allow at least 2 hours
Refreshments	Café at car park entrance; kiosk at the Visitor Centre. The Cottage Loaf pub is about 300 metres off the route – go right, up the second road in Thurstaston village
Walking conditions	Beach; good paths; one steep but very short climb. Occasionally the route along the beach can become inaccessible because of the tide. Check at the Visitor's Centre before you start

This is a walk with plenty of contrast – a beach, secluded woodland, high ground with great views, and Wirrals' only natural waterfall. Allow some time at the Visitor Centre. There's a good exhibition, helpful staff, and details of many activities for all ages. There is also a bird hide with plenty of information on what to look out for.

1. **Walk across the grass in front of the Centre to the cliff top.**

   The humps in the grass are World War II gun emplacements which have been buried rather than demolished. Kite flying is popular here and you may see hang-gliders launching off the cliffs. In front of you lie the Dee Estuary and the coast of north Wales.

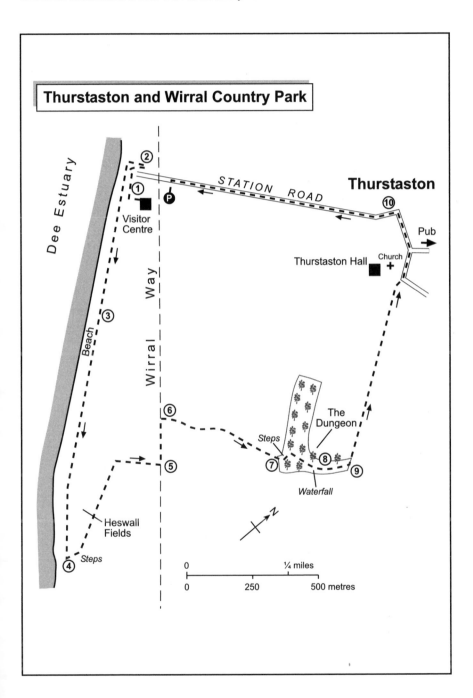

Thurstaston and Wirral Country Park

The North Hoyle windfarm is a distinctive feature off the north Wales coast, near Prestatyn. Owned by 'npower renewables', the 30 turbines are claimed to generate electricity for up to 40,000 homes. The hub of each turbine is 67 metres (220 feet) above average sea level.

Below you, at low tide, you can see small islands of grass in the mud. This is cord-grass, sometimes known by its scientific name of *Spartina maritima*. Cord-grass has a great ability to trap grains of mud and stop the flow of water. This means that mud gradually accumulates around it, and is leading to the spread of saltmarsh in many places around Britain's more southerly coasts including the Dee estuary.

2. **Go right, along the clifftop, to reach the road; go left to the bollards and then take the path to the right which soon descends to the beach.**

Our route will go left, but before doing so, notice the area to your right at the bottom of the cliffs. This was probably the site of a port called Dawpool, mentioned in several documentary records 250 or so years ago, and previously known as Redbank. No maps exist to show its exact location but there's a neat row of sandstone blocks further along that perhaps marked a jetty.

Turn left at the bottom of the cliff to walk almost a mile.

The cliffs are made of a material called boulder clay or, technically, 'till'. Vast, thick icy glaciers once covered most of Britain, including the Wirral. Glaciers actually flow, like rivers, but very slowly. As they do so, they pick up and pulverise any rocky material they come across. The material that makes up these cliffs – the boulder clay – was picked up from much further north in Britain and dumped here when the ice melted about 10,000 years ago.

As you walk along the beach you will notice pebbles of many different colours. These are broken and rounded fragments of rock mostly dragged here by the ice from the Lake District, Scotland and Ireland. How many different colours of pebble can you count?

For information on the birdlife see page 141.

3. **Continue along the beach ignoring any steps to the left.**

The cliffs and nearby area have been designated by English Nature as a Site of Special Scientific Interest (SSSI). One of their attractions is that the cliffs are constantly wearing away, due to the action of the sea at their foot. This means that trees and shrubs have little chance to grow, but many less common smaller plants are able to colonise here. This constant change to the cliffs means that the authorities have said that it

The cliffs, made from clay and rocks brought from far away

is dangerous to clamber on them. You will notice great cracks in the cliffs in places, and several areas where higher land has slipped down to the base.

4. **The cliffs gradually get lower; eventually notice a series of benches on top of cliffs which by now are very low. Just after this the cliffs finally peter out where a small stream crosses the sand towards cord-grass in the estuary. Go sharp left here, up a sandy path, next to some boulders (the path is hidden from view until you reach it). After about 20 metres ignore a forking path to the left into a field – stay on the main path.**

Heswall Fields to your left is a 40 acre/16 hectare National Trust site bought in 1978 as part of what they now call their 'Neptune Coastline Campaign'. The Trust buys up stretches of coastline whenever it can to protect it against development. So far, it owns over 710 miles of British coast.

The hawthorn hedge to the left of the path show signs of having been laid – see page 90 for more on hedge-laying.

5. **The path turns right over a stream and eventually comes to the Wirral Way. Cross to the further path and turn left.**

Looking out to sea

The railway line that once ran along here opened in 1886. The last train used it in 1962, and in 1973 the disused line became the dominant feature of the Country Park – the first designated 'Country Park' in Britain.

6. **After about 200 metres turn right, signposted to The Dungeon. Follow the pretty path gently uphill for over 500 metres, to eventually reach a wide wooded valley.**

This is The Dungeon – the name comes from an old local word meaning 'a wooded valley' – an area of old woodland, dominated by oaks. It is steep and rocky and, to the left, you can see a cave cut into the rock. It's not surprising that there are tales of smugglers using the area as place to shelter centuries ago.

7. **Cross the small bridge on your left and climb the steps a few metres later. Turn right at the top of the steps. Take care with**

young children for the next stretch; there is a steep drop to your right for a little way.

If you are interested in rocks, stop a few metres after a dip in the path, just beyond a clump of holly trees, looking down the steep bank. Here is a superb example of a geological 'fault', which occurs when two sections of rock have shifted relative to each other. Down to your right, you can see the valley walls are made of red sandstone – solid, 'blocky', and rounded. But to your left the walls are made of stone sliced into lots of thin horizontal layers – 'siltstone' (even more visible as you continue up the path). The two rocks now butt up against each other like mismatched wallpaper.

Soon you will come to a waterfall – small, and the only natural free-falling example on the Wirral (there is, though, a pretty water cascade in Walk 5). The waterfall occurs because water is only able to flow over the underlying rock – siltstone. However, Wirral's

The Dee Estuary at low tide

predominant rock is sandstone, which is porous. This means that water normally filters through it.

8. **Continue along the path, over old railway sleepers, a boardwalk, and paving slabs.**

9. **When you reach a path T-junction turn left, immediately going through a kissing gate. Stay on the same heading, through more gates, to reach Thurstaston village.**

Along the way, as the ground rises, you get great views across to Wales: the distant mountains of Snowdonia, the Great Orme near Llandudno, and, on a really clear day, Anglesey 50 miles away.

Thurstaston village is ancient and is mentioned in the Domesday Book, written in 1086. As you near St Bartholomew's Church you will notice that there is a tower in the graveyard. This is the only remains of a church built in 1820, and you can see the line where its gable end butted up against the tower. There was another ancient church before that one; the current one was built in 1886. The lychgate at the front of the church was erected in memory of Thomas Ismay, who lived in a large house nearby and died in 1899. He was founder of the White Star Line which owned the ill-fated Titanic – his son was much criticised for cowardice after surviving the sinking.

The big building behind the church is Thurstaston Hall. The extraordinary brick central section dates from the 1500s and other parts are even earlier. In the 1980s a gang of workmen found what was said to be a 'smuggler's tunnel' leading from the Hall towards the coast. The Hall is also supposed to be haunted, and the ghost once sat long enough for someone to sketch its portrait!

10. **Follow the road as it bends to the left. 100 metres after the bend look right to admire the enormous barn.**

It was built in 1862 and made of typical local materials – sandstone walls with a Welsh slate roof. It is, incidentally, also attractive at night, when it is lit up.

In about two-thirds of a mile you reach the car park on your left.

The old Thurstaston Station platforms are still visible on the coastward side of the car park. This was a single-track railway but with passing loops at some stations. The only significant accident on the whole line occurred at Thurstaston when two trains collided in 1957 and one railway employee was seriously injured.

Walk 16: Willaston

**A restored railway station – a Roman road – old buildings –
Wirral's largest windmill – an ancient hedge –
The Wirral Way – farmland – a glow-worm site**

Start and finish	Hadlow Road Station, Willaston on the B5151. Willaston is signposted from the A540
Distance	3¾ miles
Approximate time	Allow 2 hours
Refreshments	Pollard Inn; The Nag's Head; Aston's tearooms, all in Willaston
Walking conditions	Generally good paths and occasional road. The track at point 8 can be rather muddy after rain

*Allow time to look around Hadlow Road Station. It has been restored
to how it looked in 1952, when trains ran on the line between Hooton
and West Kirby. The display includes advertisements and tools; you can
see the old ticket office and look inside the signal box.*

1. **At the road entrance to the station, turn right towards the village
   centre.**

   After about 100m you pass Ash Tree Farm on your right, one of
   many very old buildings in the village. The earliest part of the
   farm, to the right, is made of sandstone and dates from the early
   1600s. The cross-wing section, made of hand-made brick, was
   added in 1697. Further along the road, also on the right, is the
   E-shaped Old Hall which, despite the 1558 date stone over the
   door, is also thought to have been built in the early 1600s.

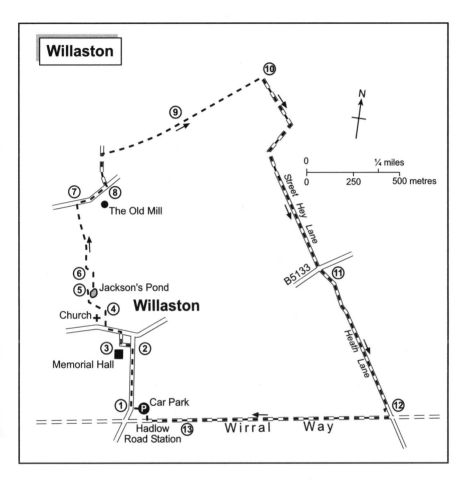

2. **Take a look at the 'Willaston' village sign a few metres on from the Hall, then cross the road onto the village green, with its copper beech tree in the centre, and aim half-left to the Memorial Hall.**

The village sign is made of 'millstone grit', a tough form of sandstone forming much of the Pennines, and also found, nearer to home, across the Dee estuary in north Wales. This type of stone was widely used for grinding grain in mills – hence the name. This particular millstone came from the windmill we'll see later on the walk.

Willaston is an ancient place known to have existed before the Domesday Book of AD1086. In the Middle Ages, it gave its name to the administrative area – known as a 'hundred' – which covered all of the Wirral. It is possible that the representatives from all the Wirral's villages met on the green, which used to be much larger than it is today.

People have been living in the area much longer than this though: several axes used by prehistoric man have been found in local fields.

A plaque on the front of the Hall shows the position of several of Willaston's noted buildings. The nearby beige building with light-brown timbers dates from 1631 and, for a while, was an inn called the Red Lion.

The copper beech, in the centre of the Green was planted in 1935 to commemorate the Silver Jubilee of King George V.

3. **Go to the main road, and cross at the pelican crossing. Go left 10 metres and then turn right to take the path alongside the churchyard.**

4. **At the end of the churchyard wall, bear diagonally left, aiming for a break in another wall about 60 metres away, signposted as a footpath. Follow this path through some trees, emerging by Jackson's Pond.**

Take a moment to look at the field to your left – it has long dips and bumps in it which extend to the other side of the tennis courts. These may be relics of old 'ridge and furrow' farming (see pages 95-6) or, more probably, of 19th century ploughing using newly invented 'steam ploughs'.

5. **Go through the gate to the right into Jackson's Pond (passing stands of reed mace or 'bulrushes'), and along the wooden walkway. Continue along the curving path to emerge at Willaston Meadow and Woodland.**

Go right to wend your way along the curving paths through the meadow, to eventually reach a wooden gate near the far left hand side.

This award-winning site is managed as a community resource by villagers. Wild flowers have been sown to create a semi-natural grass meadow. Fruit trees, and oak and beech saplings have been planted, and local children have made stretches of new hedge. A wide variety of wildlife is now attracted to the area.

There is an information board at the far gate with more about the development of the meadow and what it contains.

6. **Turn right to reach a kissing gate. Continue, over a stile, and then over another at a road.**

7. **Turn right and walk about 150m.**

There has been a mill on or near here since 1321. This mill – at 30 metres high, the largest on the Wirral – was built in 1800 and used to grind flour and, later, cattle food. It stopped being used in 1930 when the sails were severely damaged in a storm. You can see other buildings associated with the mill – the bakery, cart shed and stables – which have been turned into houses.

8. **Just after the mill, turn left along a track (there's a signpost to 'Raby'). After about 150 metres go up the stone steps to the right, over a stile and straight ahead down the side of the field.**

9. **Continue in the same direction, over or past stiles, and crossing two footbridges made of double railway sleepers.**

The large hedge to your left is ancient. Dating hedges is not a

Willaston Mill, the tallest on the Wirral

precise science but, as a rule of thumb, for each woody plant species found in a 30-metre stretch of hedge, the hedge is 100 years old. Eight species have been noted in some stretches here, suggesting the hedge is 800 years old (and maybe more). Species I have noted along the stretch you are walking include oak, hawthorn, gorse, elder, holly, rowan, hazel, sycamore and willow. The next village up the Wirral is Raby, which is thought to have been the southern limit of where Norse settlers came to live around AD900. This means the substantial hedge may once have separated Norse and Anglo-Saxon Wirral. Today it marks the boundary between Merseyside and Cheshire.

10. **Immediately after a stile and third bridge, made from a single sleeper, turn right onto a good path. Keep on the main path, which becomes a track and then a road.**

You pass by several ponds along here – marl pits. These pits were dug for their sub-soil, which was spread over the nearby land as a

Ancient oaks at the edge of Willaston's marl pits

fertiliser. The pits later filled in naturally with water. The fields off to the right were some of the earliest farming land in Willaston, in use in the Middle Ages, so the pits, which have gnarled and bent oaks growing around them, may be very old. There were complaints to the local court in the 13th century that 'dangerous' marl pits had been made at Willaston – these were dangerous to deer, which mattered far more than people at that time! (See page 58)

This road is Street Hey Lane, believed to be an old Roman road from Chester's North Gate up the Wirral. The road was archaeologically excavated in 1960, with trenches sunk in several places just before the B5133. This revealed a layer of cobbles carefully laid on a sand and clay bed.

11. **At the junction with the B5133, go straight over into Heath Lane. Continue along here for about half a mile.**

12. **Just before the road starts to narrow and rise, fork right. At the Wirral Country park noticeboard turn right to follow the Wirral Way.**

If you had turned left, under the bridge, a few hundred metres further on there is a rare site where glow-worms can be found – rangers lead walks to track them down on summer nights.

The Wirral Way was opened in 1973, and was Britain's first designated Country Park. It follows the line of the old railway from Hooton to West Kirby, which closed to rail traffic in 1962.

13. **A few hundred metres later take the right-hand fork between gateposts to arrive back at the car park.**

Walk 17: Shotwick Castle and Saughall

A medieval castle site – quaint buildings – a short visit to Wales – historic engineering of the Dee estuary – woodland – farmland

Start and finish	At the centre of Saughall, by the prominent clock tower of the Vernon Institute. Park on the road nearby (there is a car park behind the Institute but, strictly speaking, it's for visitors there). Saughall Village is signposted off the A540 Parkgate Road, about 750 metres (½ mile) south of the junction with the A5117
Distance	Just under 4 miles
Approximate time	Allow at least 2 - 2½ hours
Refreshments	Greyhound Inn in Saughall
Walking conditions	Some pavement/ paved track; woodland – short sections may sometimes be a little overgrown in summer; fields – sometimes muddy but when I last walked the route, after a wet period in winter, my boots were pristine; it just depends on whether the fields are ploughed or churned up by livestock

This walk is a cracker, one of my favourites. It's very rural, with some great views, and there's loads of interest along the way. It takes in what I think is one of the most evocative places in our area – the site of Shotwick Castle.

You may not immediately think of Saughall (pronounced 'Sorgle' by the way) as being part of the Wirral, but it falls within the ancient administrative area of the 'hundred of Wirral', which stretched down to Blacon Point a couple of miles further south, towards Chester. Saughall today is a curious mix of recent housing and quaint farm buildings and cottages. The map on the noticeboard by the clock tower gives much local information. I don't have space to mention all the buildings but a few to look out for include the Vicarage (opposite the entrance to the Institute's car park) much visited by the composer Sir Edward Elgar (see illustration), The Swinging Gate (situated at the crossroads),

The blue plaque remembering Sir Edward Elgar at the Vicarage

built in the 1500s and until fairly recently a pub; on the right just after the pub, Bridge Farm, a timbered building that has been extended both upwards and to the left, with the brickwork painted to match the timber; and, later on the right, pretty Pine Cone Cottage.

1. **From the Vernon Institute head downhill, along Sea Hill Road.**

   The road name gives a clue to the past. When you drop down the steeper part of the hill you are descending the old bank of the River Dee which used to run all along this side of the estuary to Chester. For centuries, shifting sands meant that the river was hard to navigate, especially for large ships, so in 1737 the course was diverted from a point near Neston to the other side of the estuary, and partly canalised. So, from the bottom of the hill, you are walking where the river, and tidal seawater, once flowed.

   Where the road bends slightly left, by a stone marked 'Chester 1995' you enter Wales.

2. **Go over the hump-backed bridge and, soon, take the tarmac track to your left, to double back on yourself. Reach the main cycleway and turn left.**

   Notice the milepost of the National Cycle Network, one of four different designs for the roughly 1000 such posts scattered across

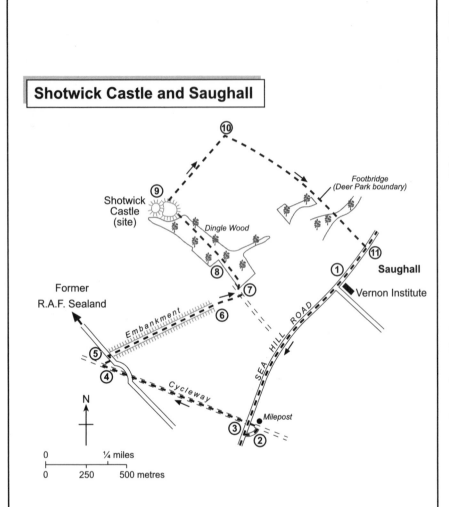

Shotwick Castle and Saughall

the country. This design is called 'Fossil tree' and the images on the 'trunk' span millions of years of earth history from ancient sea creatures – trilobites – at the base, to the end of fossil fuels at the top.

The 'Fossil tree' milepost

3. **Go under the bridge and continue along the cycleway, past metal gates at a farm, and under another bridge.**

You are walking on a disused railway track, built on an embankment to avoid the track becoming flooded on the low-lying land. If you get a chance to look at the soil on any part of this low-lying section you may notice there are hardly any stones in it – the fine soil is alluvium, once deposited by the Dee into the estuary. It is very fertile so crops are usually grown here; last time I saw a field of leeks - rather appropriate as it's the national symbol of Wales.

4. **Soon after the second bridge, take the turn right, by another National Cycle Network milepost, to meet a road. Turn left.**

Some way ahead, to your half-left, you can see the buildings of former RAF Sealand, the hangars of which have recently been listed as being of historic importance. The aerodrome started in 1917 as a private flying school, but was quickly taken over by the Royal Flying Corps to become a training base for First World War pilots. Later it was used by the US Air Force and then became a maintenance unit for RAF electronic equipment. The RAF base closed a few years ago but Dara Electronics carries on similar work there today for both civil and military customers.

5. **After about 75 metres take the signed path right, opposite the white house, over a stile. Go straight ahead, along the wide,**

grassy embankment, with a fence to your left and a line of low hawthorn trees to your right.

Once the Dee was diverted, a number of embankments were built over the following 180 years to prevent flooding and reclaim the land for agricultural use (hence the local village name Sealand, i.e. 'land from the sea'). This embankment was built in 1790 and, judging by what has been thrown up by the molehills and badger setts, comprises large amounts of sand.

6. **Continue to the end of the embankment, where there is a pretty scattering of Scots pine and larch. Cross the metal footbridge and stile (welcome back to England here by the way!). Walk initially with the slow stream to your right; when it bends right go straight ahead to a kissing gate and a track.**

7. **Turn left, then right just before a gate, over a stile. Immediately fork left, up the bank, then go left following a clear narrow path**

The old embankment (left) runs past a pretty stand of conifers

along the top of the slope (later, ignore a path coming in from the right).

You have just clambered up the old bank of the Dee, into the woods. The trees and shrubs here include ash, beech, elm, sycamore, hawthorn, oak, and blackthorn. Non-native rhododendrons can look attractive but need cutting back from time to time; otherwise they can overwhelm everything around them destroying the woodland.

8. **Cross a wooden footbridge, after which the path leaves the edge of the bank. After more woodland, another bridge, and a sometimes-overgrown path through bracken, you reach the site of Shotwick Castle.**

Nothing remains of the structure of the castle today, but the massive earthworks, including an inner and outer moat, suggest a very substantial building. A motte and bailey castle was built here first by the conquering Normans, 900 years or so ago. The castle was later rebuilt in stone to defend the English-Welsh border and was used by English kings to support their attacks on Wales in the 12th and 13th centuries. It may have been pentagonal in shape and was built right against the estuary so that ships could moor alongside it. Today, the river is gone but osiers (willows) sit in the damp ground below the castle site. In 1327, a deer park was created at Shotwick and, with the threat from Wales gone, the castle was turned into a hunting lodge. It never ceases to amaze me how, very frequently, every trace of large old buildings has disappeared – with the materials used elsewhere. Recycling is certainly not new!

I suggest you spend time wandering over the dips and mounds of the earthworks but you may wish to head first for the interpretation board, which has illustrations and more information, found by keeping to the right-hand edge of the field to reach a kissing gate.

Keep your eye open for buzzards – I have often seen them wheeling in the skies around here.

9. **From the kissing gate walk gently uphill, through another**

kissing gate and on to a third
(where there is yet another
one, tucked in the hedge to
your left). Don't go through
this third gate but go right,
keeping the dense hedge on
your left.

10. From that third kissing gate
you keep in the same direction
all the way back to Saughall.
Along the way you go through
several more kissing gates,
cross two stiles at a footbridge,
and through a narrow strip of
woodland.

Part of the moat that once
surrounded Shotwick Castle

Do look right from time to time, taking in the fine view across to
the hills of Wales.

The footbridge goes over a stream and substantial ditch. This
marks the boundary of the former deer park, where Edward the
'Black Prince', father to Richard II, hunted in the 1300s. The ditch
would have helped keep the deer in the park, and there would have
been a fence too. The buildings up the field to your left include
'Parkgate House', marking the park's entrance.

11. When you reach the road at Saughall turn right to head back to
the car (keeping an eye out for more of Saughall's quaint
buildings along the way).

Walk 18: West Kirby and Red Rocks

Superb views – a Marine Lake – sailing and sand yachting – sand dunes – Natterjack toads – an internationally famous golf course

Start and finish	On South Parade, West Kirby. Park on the road or in the nearby supermarket pay-and-display. Regular trains and buses also run to the town
Distance	Up to 4 miles split into two loops, one of 1½ miles , the other of 2½ miles
Approximate time	Allow 2½ hours in total. First loop 1 hour; second loop 1½ hours (as there's lots to see)
Refreshments	Numerous pubs, restaurants and cafés in West Kirby
Walking conditions	Solid, level ground underfoot for the shorter loop; firm sand, board walks and an optional short section of rock for the other loop

This seaside walk has so much going for it. If you like watching other people being active then admire the sailors and sand-yachters. If you want a bit more tranquility, the dunes are lovely, particularly on a sunny day. You can also potter on the beach or explore rock pools. And all the time you've got great views. All in all, one of my favourites!

1. **Start by walking a circuit of West Kirby Marine Lake (I suggest walking clockwise, to get the best views).**

The circuit is accessible at all but the highest tides. As well as great views there is always entertainment from watching the various

One of the pools in the dunes

activities on the lake, which include wind-surfing, sailing and kayaking. If you think the windsurfers look fast you may like to know that a world windsurfing speed record was set on the lake in 1991 and held for two years: over 42 knots (almost 50 mph!). Back home you can watch the activity on the Lake in real time at: http://www.wirralcam.org/westkirby.shtml

The lake was built in 1899 and, as well as offering an attractive leisure facility, provides protection from erosion for the shore. The coming of the railway from Birkenhead to West Kirby in 1878 meant that, by the time the lake opened, West Kirby was already an attractive destination for day-trippers enjoying the long sandy beach.

2. **For the second loop, start opposite Dee lane, by the West Kirby Beach noticeboard. Walk along the beach. 50 metres after the last garden on the right, take the steps up the dune. Follow the obvious path along the ridge; later it drops slightly.**

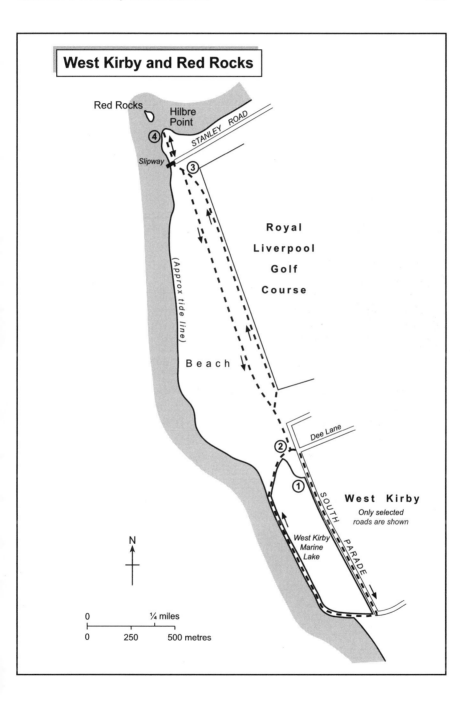

You are walking through the Red Rocks Marsh Nature Reserve, a mix of sand dunes and brackish (slightly salty) pools. The latter are home to Natterjack toads which, because of their rarity, are protected by the law. They breed in warm water which they find in the shallow pools ('slacks') that form in the dunes. The toads have a distinctive yellow stripe down their back, but are usually only seen at night. There are also many birds and interesting plants to be seen through this area – interpretation boards at each end of this section give more information.

The Royal Liverpool Golf Course to your right was built in 1869, on what was then the racecourse of the Liverpool Hunt Club (Wirral has abounded in race courses – see also Walks 7, 10, 14, 19). It was the venue for The Open Championship in 2006, won by Tiger Woods, and is set to host it again in 2014.

What looks like a white lighthouse is a distinctive feature on the horizon – but actually it is a folly, built as an attractive addition to the house, and was never used for guiding ships. But one of Hoylake's original lighthouses, an octagonal brick tower, still stands in the town.

3. **When you reach the end of the boardwalk, continue over rocks and a sandy path to reach a slipway. Continue to the left of a wall to the corner of the peninsula – Hilbre Point.**

Here you have great views out to Liverpool Bay, including the Burbo Bank windfarm to your half-right and North Hoyle windfarm to the half-left (see pages 98 and 110). To your left is Hilbre Island. Towards the left end of the island is the bird observatory and at the right tip is the Old Lifeboat Station. See Walk 20 for more information.

To your right is the town of Hoylake, its name derived from Hoyle Lake, a deep water channel where ships used to anchor if they couldn't, or didn't want to, use the Dee Estuary with its shifting sands. In 1690 King William II set sail from here with 10,000 troops to take part in the Battle of the Boyne near Drogheda, Ireland.

At low tides you may see sand-yachts whizzing around to your right. Three-wheeled 'yachts' use sails to power across the sand –

The beach here is always a favourite with children. Hilbre Island is in the background

the world record is 116 mph! You may also see 'parakarting' where buggies are pulled along by small parachutes. An area is designated for these activities, starting 300 metres offshore and covering about 8 square miles – the largest such area in the country.

Ahead of you lie the raised Red Rocks – worth wading to at low tide to explore the rock pools (but take care, the rocks can be slippery). The rock and mudflats are a popular spot for bird watchers, attracting many different bird species feasting on the lugworms and shellfish. At high tides you may also spot fishermen marooned on the rocks in the hope of making a catch.

4. **Return to point 3, but instead of taking the boardwalk along the back of the dunes, fork right taking the obvious level path on the lower land.**

Along the way you will pass more pools which toads inhabit.

Walk 19: Leasowe

A lighthouse – a hovercraft tale – coastline – sand dunes – hay meadow – the origins of 'The Derby' horse race

Start and finish	Leasowe lighthouse (off the A551, at the junction of Pasture Road and Leasowe Road, Moreton)
Distance	Up to 4 miles
Approximate time	Allow at least 2 hours, but it is easy to cut short
Refreshments	None en route
Walking conditions	Level ground, suitable for pushchairs, etc, except the optional eastern section using sandy/grassy paths over low hills

This is a route for all the family with easy, mostly flat walking.

There is plenty to see but you can make it as short as you want by re-tracing your route at any time.

The walking route is within the boundary of North Wirral Coastal Park. Many of the Park's features are mentioned on this walk but you may also like to wander round Moreton Conservation Area (to your left as you face the sea from the lighthouse), which is a wildlife haven. It includes a pond, reed-beds and a wildflower meadow. The whole of the North Wirral Foreshore has been designated as a Site of Special Scientific Interest because of the variety of wild birds it attracts – especially noticeable at low tides as they look for food in the sand and mudflats.

The lighthouse has a '1763' date-stone above the doorway and the initials 'M.W.G.' after the then mayor of Liverpool, William Gregson. You can make out bricks under the whitewashed exterior – this is the earliest brick-built lighthouse in the country and is 30 metres high. It is regularly open to visitors who can climb the 130 cast-iron steps to the top. Originally there was another light on the seashore and, by aligning the two lights, ships could find the entrance to the channel that led to the Port of Liverpool. But the shore light collapsed, so a replacement was built on Bidston Hill in 1771, and ships' captains then aligned the Bidston and Leasowe lights.

1. **After viewing the lighthouse, take the tarmac path up to Wallasey Embankment. Turn right.**

The 3-mile-long embankment is just one of various types of sea defence that protect the north Wirral coast. Behind the embankment lie 18 square kilometres of land below the level of highest tides. The rows

The lighthouse

of concrete cubes in the car park are leftover examples of one of the types of sea defence which line the shore at various places along this coast.

The 25 wind turbines ahead are part of the 'Burbo Bank' windfarm, 7 km offshore. Its Danish owners claim that, if they were able to operate at maximum capacity, they would produce enough power for 80,000 homes (though in reality every wind farm operates at very substantially below maximum capacity because of the vagaries of our weather). Each turbine measures 137 metres from average sea level to the tip of the highest blade.

Slightly left, on a clear day, you can see the Liverpool Bay Douglas oil and gas complex in the far distance. Gas extracted from below the seabed is sent via a 34 km pipeline to a processing terminal at Point of Ayr, North Wales. Meanwhile, oil is piped 20 km from the drilling platform to a double-hulled supertanker permanently moored away from shipping lanes. Here the oil is transferred into tankers for international export.

The shore here was one terminus of the world's first hovercraft passenger service – and possibly the shortest-lived! The idea was to run a regular service between Leasowe embankment and Rhyl in north Wales. The service started on July 14th 1962 but on the 14th September that year the craft lost an engine and then got badly damaged in a storm. The service never operated again.

After almost a mile you pass Leasowe Castle to your right (you cannot access it from the path). The original sandstone Castle was built in 1593, not as a defensive structure but possibly in connection with a horse race course built nearby (there are several former race courses on the Wirral – see also Walks 7, 10, 14 and 18). This course was made by the Earl of Derby and was the location of the first Derby race, now famously run at Epsom. The Castle soon became a ruin and was given a common name for such ruins – Mockbeggar Hall. The nearby shore is called Mockbeggar Wharf today.

The building was later restored and extended, and there are still hints of the past inside: the 'Star Chamber' is impressive with wood-panelled walls (the panelling actually came from the Palace of Westminster in 1836) and large hanging tapestries depicting the four seasons.

2. **At the wide bay drop down to the shore, if the tide allows (or stay on the path if you prefer).**

The bay is not an ancient feature. Unlike the rest of this coast this stretch has never been owned by the local authority so it did not benefit from the first coastal protection schemes. In the first half of the 20th century the dunes that covered this stretch receded by 85 metres, forming the bay. The breakwaters of piled-up boulders in the bay were constructed in the 1970s and 80s to limit the damage, and further boulders line the back of the shore. Most of the boulders are made of limestone that was formed on the seabed; you will quickly spot fossils of shellfish and coral in the rock.

3. **At the end of the bay re-join the main path and very soon fork right to look at the information board at this end of the car park which contains details of local wildlife. Rejoin the sea wall path**

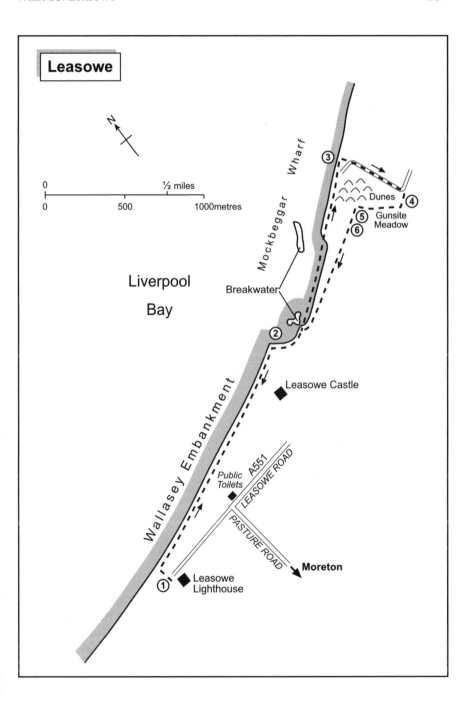

Leasowe

N

| 0 | | ½ miles |
| 0 | 500 | 1000metres |

Mockbeggar Wharf

③

Dunes ④

⑤ Gunsite
⑥ Meadow

Liverpool

Breakwater

Bay

②

Leasowe Castle

Wallasey Embankment

Public
Toilets

A551

LEASOWE ROAD

PASTURE ROAD

Moreton

① Leasowe
Lighthouse

Leasowe Bay (Photo: Adam King)

and continue to the far end of the parking area to a gap in the wall on the right by a National Cycle Network sign.

If you wish to keep to level ground then retrace your steps from this point; otherwise turn right, away from the sea wall, and go down the access road until you reach a car park.

4. Go across the tarmacked area, through a wooden kissing gate at the end and along a short stretch of path to reach an information board which tells you about Gunsite Meadow.

This hay meadow is rich with wildflowers in summer, and is named after anti-aircraft guns sited here during World War II.

5. Take the diagonal path across the meadow, passing just left of trees, to reach another kissing gate. Immediately after it turn right for 30 metres to look at another information board, on your left. Then go left along the path, initially on bricks, and soon join the main path, uphill. In a few metres note the steps uphill to your left – you will want to take these later. First though,

continue on the main path to view the dunes (and another information board).

You may wish to take a detour to wander around the dunes, which are an increasingly threatened habitat nationally. These ones are particularly vulnerable as the coastal defences stop them from being replenished with sand blown from the shore. They are home to a number of animals and plants, many rare, which are mentioned on the boards.

The commonest plant you will see on the dunes is marram grass and it is very important for the preservation of dunes. The plant has an incredible ability to grow really long roots, so no matter how high the dunes get, it can still tap down into the water beneath the sand (marram has been known to sit on 30 metre high dunes). It can also spread a long way horizontally creating a new bud whenever the sand overwhelms it. This network of roots and shoots helps bind the sand dunes together, limiting erosion. You can see areas of the dune that have been fenced off; new marram is being planted here to encourage the dunes to stabilise.

6. **Return to the steps and, at the top, continue along this path. Keep to the main path along the centre of ridge.**

This area is known as the 'Bund'. It is a lovely meadow today but, amazingly, used to be a rubbish tip. Skylarks nest here and you may see them soaring upwards and hovering, singing excitedly.

Eventually rejoin the path above the shore and retrace your steps to the lighthouse.

Walk 20: Hilbre Island

**Great views – an old lifeboat station and signal station –
rock caves and an arch – wildlife including seals –
a weather station you can check at home –
where dinosaurs once roamed**

Start and finish	The slipway near the north end of the West Kirby Marine Lake. Parking, buses and railway station nearby
Distance	About 4 miles
Approximate time	Allow 1 hour each way, plus stops including plenty of time on Hilbre. Allow extra walking time if you have children
Refreshments	None on the island; take a picnic – stop anywhere on Middle Eye or Hilbre to eat while enjoying great views. There are, incidentally, public loos – eco-friendly composting ones! – on Hilbre
Walking conditions	Flat, over sand, shingle and occasional rock, which may be slippery in one or two places; grassy paths. It should be possible to keep your feet dry! If there is a strong wind against you, it can make walking quite tiring. Don't attempt the walk in poor visibility

Visiting Hilbre is a memorable day out, with lots to see, rock-pools, caves and beaches to explore, and masses of wildlife. Plan your visit around the tide times as Hilbre is cut off for several hours per day. Plan either to walk there and back during one low tide, or to stay there while the tide comes in and goes out again.

A notice board by the slipway gives full information on the tides as well as telling you much more about the island. Alternatively, call the

Wirral Country Park Visitor Centre on 0151 648 4371 or 3884. You may like to time your visit for when the Old Telegraph Station is opened by The Friends of Hilbre – it has interesting displays on the island's history and wildlife. See www.hilbreisland.org.uk for details.

1. **Do not walk directly from West Kirby to Hilbre as the sand is unsafe. Instead, walk towards the left-hand island, called Little Eye.**

Hilbre Island is the largest of four islands. Tanskey Rocks to your half-left are largely buried in the sand and invisible; then there's Little Eye which you are initially aiming for. A little way to the right is Middle Eye (also known as Little Hilbre), and immediately to its right is Hilbre Island itself. They are all areas of sandstone rock left sticking up 10,000 years ago after the melting of mighty glaciers that had carved out the Dee Estuary.

The islands have been occupied since the Stone Age, and there was a Christian community based on them 1000 or more years ago. A cell of monks, enjoying the peace and isolation, used Hilbre until 1536.

As you cross the sand you will notice millions of little mounds of sand. These are the casts of lugworms who swallow the sand they live in, digesting the organic material, and ejecting the rest to make the cast. Lugworms, as well as other sand-living animals such as ragworms and various molluscs (shellfish), attract numerous birds to feed, which is why the Dee Estuary has been designated a Site of Special Scientific Interest. Birds that are easy to spot include curlews – with long downward-curving beaks; oystercatchers with red beaks, black upper body and white lower body; and redshanks – smaller and lighter-coloured than oystercatchers and with red beak and legs. Other important birds here include grey plovers, knots, dunlin and bar-tailed godwit.

2. **When you reach Little Eye turn right and make your way to Middle Eye.**

Middle Eye has lovely grassy paths which you reach from steps on the right-hand side next to a wave-cut tunnel in the rocks. On the left side of the island is Smuggler's Cave – the islands were said to be the haunt of smugglers and wreckers in the past. And on Hilbre itself you can find Lady's Cave where, legend says, a dying girl was cast up after throwing herself from a ship to avoid an arranged marriage (take care if you try to find the caves; the rocks are very slippery).

3. **Continue to Hilbre Island, past rock-pools where you may find crabs, to a path starting on the left-hand side of the cliff. (You may wish to first wander along the base of the island, perhaps visiting Lion Rock, which is roughly lion shaped, and which sits in a bay known locally as 'Niffy Bay' because it sometimes pongs a bit!)**

The islands' rocks were formed over 200 million years ago when what is now Wirral was part of a vast desert. Footprints of a prehistoric reptile called cheirotherium have been found on Hilbre (and at Storeton Quarry – Walk 7) and a cast of a print can been seen in the Old Telegraph Station when it is open.

The Old Telegraph Station

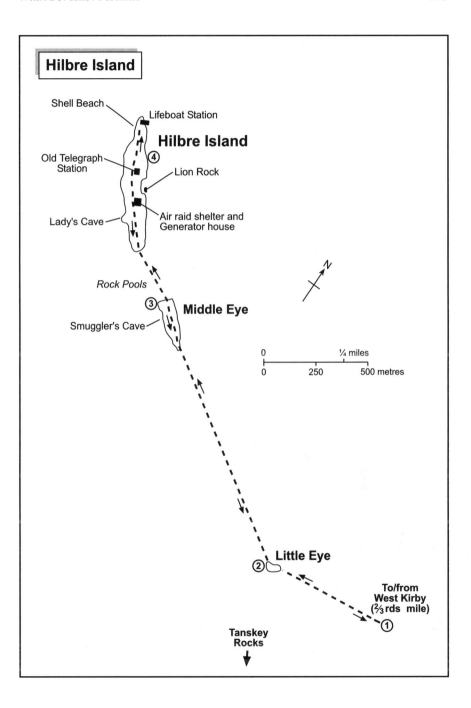

Hilbre Island

Shell Beach

Lifeboat Station

Hilbre Island

④

Old Telegraph Station

Lion Rock

Lady's Cave

Air raid shelter and Generator house

N

Rock Pools

③ **Middle Eye**

Smuggler's Cave

0   ¼ miles
0   250   500 metres

② **Little Eye**

To/from West Kirby (⅔rds mile)

①

Tanskey Rocks

Along the path notice mounds of grass on your right, one with a low brick chimney sticking up. They held an air raid shelter during World War II and also an electrical generator. From here, a cable led to Middle Eye on which structures had been built with holes in the top. Lights shone through the holes to deceive German bomber aircraft that these were the factories of Liverpool.

In three places on the island, including behind a wooden fence on the right along the main path, you can glimpse wire cages which are open at one end. These are Heligoland traps used to catch birds for recording and ringing before being released, in order to track their movements. There are several properties on the east side of the island. One is a bird observatory, another is occupied by the island's ranger. Some are privately leased and one is owned by the Mersey Canoe Club.

The path takes you to a white round-ended building, the Old Telegraph Station. Built in 1841, it was part of a chain of signalling stations between Liverpool with Holyhead, sending messages about

The old lifeboat station

shipping by relay along the coast. The next Wirral signal station in the chain was on Bidston Hill.

Immediately before the Old Telegraph Station is a tall mast. This is a radar station, a webcam and a weather station, part of the Liverpool Bay Coastal Observatory. When you get back home, log onto the Proudman Oceanographic Laboratory website (http://coastobs.pol.ac.uk/cobs/met/hilbre/) to get up-to-the-minute weather reports from the island, including wind speed and temperature, plus current webcam images.

To your left are steps from the bottom of which, with care, you can work your way round to Shell Beach. It has rock pools and is backed by attractive Victorian stonework designed to prevent erosion. Near the steps is one of two shell middens found on the islands – a mound of discarded shells from edible shellfish, left by Middle Stone Age (Mesolithic) inhabitants of the islands, some time between about 10,000 and 5,500 years ago.

Hilbre Island from the sands

Keep your eye on the water around the island: you are almost certain to see the heads of Atlantic grey seals bobbing around. They are also a common sight on the sandbanks in the distance towards the Welsh coast.

Up to three wind farms are visible from the island – to your half-right is Burbo Bank with 25 wind turbines, to the half-left is North Hoyle, which was Britain's first offshore wind-farm (30 turbines) and , visible to the far left on a clear day is Rhyl Flats (25 turbines).

Continue to the far tip of the island where you will find the remains of a lifeboat station, used until 1939. Originally twinned with Hoylake Lifeboat station, it was quicker at low tide for the Hoylake-based crew to travel to Hilbre and launch a boat there than to launch from the mainland. Sadly the slipway is being broken up by strong seas but at the bottom end you can just make out there are two trackways, one straight ahead and the other off to the left – a switch mechanism enabled the crew to use the appropriate track for the tide conditions.

To the left-hand side of the slipway is a deep groove in the rock, with a pipe running along the bottom. This is a part of a tide gauge. It is vital that ships going in and out of the Mersey know exactly how much draught (the depth of water needed to float the ship) is available. The tide gauge gives this information precisely and up to the minute.

4. **Return using the outward route.**

Walk 21: Landican and Little Storeton

Ancient lanes – an air crash site – farmland – pretty
hamlets – old buildings – old farming methods

Start and finish	Torrington Drive, next to the roundabout where the B5138 (Pensby Road) meets the A551 (Barnston Road), ½ mile south of the main entrance to Arrowe Country Park
Distance	4 miles
Approximate time	Allow 2 to 2½ hours
Refreshments	Basset Hound pub in Thingwall
Walking conditions	Some good tracks and road. Some of the fields can be wet or muddy, especially the first half-mile of the route in winter – wellies or good boots are recommended. To avoid this section, take Landican Road from the start point to join the route before point 3 in Landican

This route passes through three quaint hamlets, and uses some ancient lanes. Most of the time you are surrounded by fields, so it has a very rural feel.

1. Take the footpath by the roundabout, signed to 'Landican'. Keep to the left-hand field boundary, between some stone gateposts. Later, cross a footbridge then a stile and continue straight across the field. At the far side go through the broken hedge-line, keeping in the same direction, walking with a line of low trees to your right. Reach a pond and take the stile (very broken at the time of writing) on its left-hand side.

2. Keeping the hedge on your right, head towards the far right-hand corner of the field but, before the corner, drop down to the right

to pick up a farm track, and turn left. Continue to a road and turn right.

Landican is a very old Wirral settlement. It is mentioned in the Domesday Book of 1086 and at that time included a priest, nine villagers and four Frenchmen! (The latter would have come here as a result of the Norman Conquest 20 years beforehand). I love the quaint mix of farm buildings in the hamlet, such as Farm View with its dwelling built onto the end of the brick barn (on your left as you come down the farm track). The road you are walking down is sunk below the level of the land to the side, due to centuries of use. There was once a stone wall along the bank to your right – see how the roots of mature trees have wrapped themselves around the remaining stones.

3. **After 150 metres take the track signposted 'Public Bridleway to Storeton' to the right. You stay on this good path – an old route known as Landican Lane – for 1½ miles.**

This little lane, lined with old oaks, would have given access to the fields for the people of Landican over centuries. Records of 1846 show that, as well as producing oats, wheat, potatoes and turnips, many of the fields were growing clover. Clover was a valuable crop for feeding sheep and cattle; it was also an important fertiliser in the days before mass-produced agricultural chemicals – bacteria in clover's roots can convert nitrogen in the air into a form that other crops can use for growth.

After just over half a mile (almost one kilometre) you reach a left-hand bend followed by a

The memorial at Prenton to the US airmen killed in an air crash

gentle downhill stretch. The area around here was the site of Wirral's worst air crash, in 1944. An American Liberator aircraft was flying from Northern Ireland to Wiltshire when it exploded in mid-air. Wreckage was widely scattered but the bulk of it fell in the fields around this part of Landican Lane – there are still visible depressions in the fields where it struck. 24 US airmen lost their lives and a memorial to them has been erected in Brook Way, Prenton. The cause was never firmly established but an on-board explosion or a lightning strike were possible reasons; enemy action was ruled out.

Continue, going over Prenton Brook and crossing under the Bidston-Wrexham railway and, later, the M53, to eventually reach a road at Little Storeton.

This is a pretty corner of an ancient village. Look up the road that runs left. Grange Cottages, the row of houses on the left, are made of Storeton sandstone, quarried in the woods three-quarters of a mile to the east. Storeton stone is much paler than the red sandstone you find elsewhere on the Wirral, and was a popular building stone. The village smithy once stood at the far end of this row of houses.

At the point where you reach the road note the cast iron Millennium Milepost, one of 1000 created across the UK in the year 2000 for the National Cycle Network. The circular plate towards the top carries letters and numbers. These were part of a Millennium Time Trail and you could 'collect' the design by 'brass-rubbing' it. Piecing together a selection of these rubbings enabled you to solve a puzzle. The design is one of four for the posts around the country. This one is called 'Cockerel' (no, I don't understand either!).

If you wish, wander 150m down the road to glimpse Storeton Hall across a field by looking over the hedge to your left (more information on page 57). Otherwise…..

4. **15 metres later, take the stile on the right and follow the path over the motorway bridge.**

I've often seen large brown buzzards on the ground here or wheeling in the sky above me.

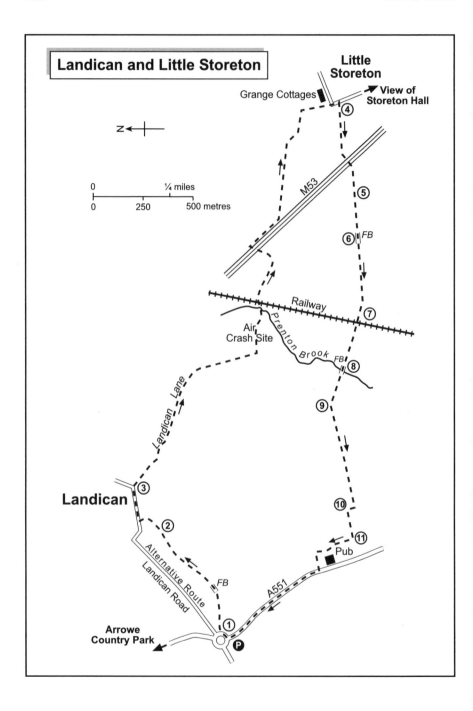

Landican and Little Storeton

Little Storeton

Grange Cottages

View of Storeton Hall

④

⑤

⑥ *FB*

N

0   ¼ miles
0   250   500 metres

M53

Railway

Air Crash Site

Prenton Brook

⑦

FB ⑧

⑨

Landican Lane

Landican

③

②

⑩

⑪

Pub

Alternative Route

Landican Road

FB

A551

①

Arrowe Country Park

P

5. **After the bridge, continue, with the fence on your left.**

6. **At the far side of the field cross a footbridge and stile, then take the clear path that goes half-right, eventually going under two sets of electricity cables.**

7. **Reach the railway – cross with care! Continue straight ahead along a narrow path.**

The track was opened in 1896 as part of the 'Dee and Birkenhead Railway'. There used to be a station 400 metres to your left – hence the road between Barnston and Storeton is 'Station Road'. The station closed to passengers in 1951. Next to the station there was once a brick-making yard, including large circular kilns to bake the bricks.

Notice the first stone gatepost you come to, about 20 metres after the track. It bears a symbol – a horizontal line with an arrow underneath. This is an Ordnance Survey 'cut benchmark' symbol – indicating a spot where the O.S. took a precise measurement of the height above sea level to help compile their maps.

8. **Go down a bank, over the stream and a stile and then half-right, diagonally up the hillside, to then walk to the right of some ponds and bushes. At the end of these, go straight ahead to cross a stile by a metal gate.**

The ponds you pass are some of hundreds that stand out on maps, dotted all over the Wirral. Many of these were dug as marl pits in past centuries. Subsoil was dug and spread over surrounding fields; the nutrients from this subsoil were another way of increasing the soil's fertility, a method known to have been used by the Romans. These pits later filled naturally with water to form ponds. Similar pits were also dug in places to obtain the clay for brick-making.

9. **Walk with the hedge to your right for two fields to reach a stile and path between hedges. Follow this path over another stile, to bend sharp right.**

10. **After 50m reach a track; turn left.**

A barley field at Little Storeton

11. Reach a sunken lane. Turn right and stay on this to reach the main road.

You pass Manor Barn on your left – notice the water trough hollowed out of a block of sandstone, a water-pump and the three-step sandstone mounting block for getting onto horses.

Go right to return to the start.

Walk 22: Backford and The Wirral Canal

An historic road – a canal, boats and bridges – old buildings – farmland

Start and finish	Small car park by the telephone box in Backford which is up Church Lane, off the A41 (signposted 'Backford') , about 3 miles north of Chester
Distance	4¼ miles
Approximate time	Allow 2¼ hours
Refreshments	None en route; the Bunbury Arms, Stoak, is a nice pub if you extend the canal walk by 1km/0.6 mile each way
Walking conditions	Mostly flat, on good surfaces. 1 mile across field-paths

This is a gentle, rural walk with a 'transport' theme. The late 18th century was a period of great change in the Britain as the industrial revolution took hold and the country's transport network was transformed. This walk follows two features of that developing transport system – a road and a canal.

Centuries earlier, Backford had marked the southern limit of the administrative region, known as the 'hundred', which covered the Wirral.

You may like to take some bread to feed the ducks and moorhens you are sure to come across on the canal.

1. **Facing the road from the car park, go left (passing an ancient oak at the end of the car park), and past the church.**

Part of the church dates back to the 1200s – you can still see the original old sandstone stonework at the opposite end of the church to the tower. The tower was added in about 1500 and is one of four within a 10-mile radius of Chester built to an identical plan; the others are at Shotwick, Handley and Tattenhall. Note the gargoyles on Backford church's tower and also the eight pinnacles on top – if you do Walk 25 through Shotwick you'll see the pinnacles are missing on Shotwick's tower, probably knocked down during religious upheavals in the 16th century.

Go left again at the A41. Continue for 800m/half a mile, passing Rake Lane.

Rake is an old local word, of Scandinavian origin, meaning a lane (much of Wirral is believed to have been settled by Norsemen after they had been driven out of Ireland in the 10th century AD).

The A41 (as well as the A540 running along west Wirral) was a 'turnpike', opened in 1787, leading up the peninsula from Chester. Turnpikes were roads operated by business trusts that built and maintained them in exchange for tolls charged to users. Previously the cost of maintaining roads had to be met by the local community but transferring the costs to road-users, via the trusts, meant rapid growth in the quantity and quality of roads. The improved network was a great force for economic expansion across Britain.

Horse-drawn passenger coaches frequently used this important road between Chester and the ferries across the Mersey at Eastham and Birkenhead. A tollgate and toll house were situated on the opposite of the road, immediately before the bridge you are about to go over, but there is no sign of the gate and house today.

2. **Cross Backford Bridge over the canal, then go down the steps on your left, and continue ahead at the bottom (note the number '133' on the bridge before you leave it).**

This section of the Shropshire Union Canal was known as the Wirral Canal when opened in 1795 by the Ellesmere Canal Company. They wanted a freight link from the textile-producing communities in Shropshire (around Ellesmere) and mid-Wales, to the Dee and Mersey. At the time, there was no village where the canal met the Mersey; the settlement that grew up there became known as 'Ellesmere Port'. The great civil engineer Thomas Telford planned the canal using a winding route that followed the land's contours,

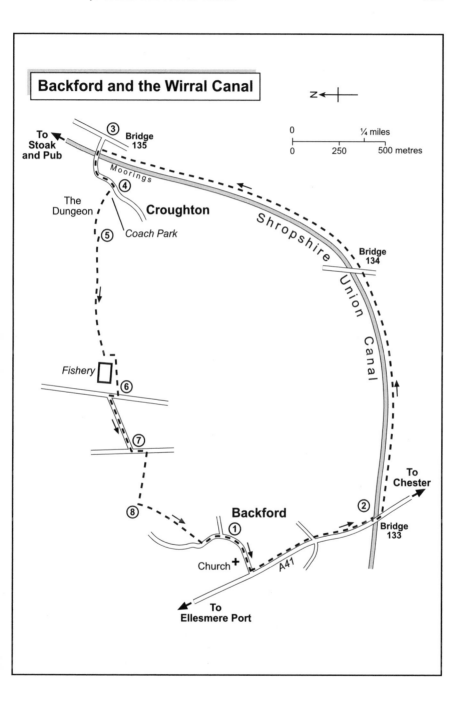

Backford and the Wirral Canal

avoiding any climbs or falls. This made locks unnecessary, speeding the journey of the canal 'flyboats', and making the route very popular for passenger traffic to and from Chester.

The valley that Telford's route followed is known as the 'Backford Gap' or 'Deva Spillway' and was probably carved by meltwater from glaciers plunging south at the end of the last ice age, about 10,000 years ago.

Each bridge is numbered. You have joined at Bridge 133 – Bridge 1 is in Wolverhampton, 67 miles away (the canal became linked to the industrial heartlands of the Midlands in the 19th century).

As you walk along this section notice the mature willows and large stands of common reed on the opposite bank, providing a lovely background sound as they rustle in the wind.

Fishing near Bridge 134 on the 'Wirral Canal'

Go under Bridge 134 (Caughall Bridge) and continue on the towpath.

Look for grooves on the brickwork on the inside edge of this and other canal bridges. These were carved by ropes used by horses to

tow the canal boats. Also, notice the opposite side of the bridges reinforced by large blocks of stone to protect against knocks from canal boats.

Rope marks on a bridge from when horses pulled the narrowboats

Chester Zoo is at the top of the hill to your right. In still weather, boat owners moored on the canal can sometimes hear strange animal noises drifting through the air.

Continue, past a long section of boat moorings on the opposite bank.

3. **At Bridge 135 climb to the lane, cross the bridge and continue walking into Croughton. (For the pub at Stoak, continue on the towpath to Bridge 136. Cross over the canal and continue for 400m; the pub is on your right).**

Croughton (pronounced 'Craw-tun' by the way) is an ancient village mentioned in the Domesday Book of 1086. There are several old houses and barns here.

4. **After 250 metres look for a footpath to the right, over a footbridge, by a coach yard (another 'transport' link on this walk!). Walk up the yard (try to keep to the right-hand side, but it may be blocked by vehicles). At the top corner of the yard, cross the stile and continue ahead, passing a steep-sided sandy valley called 'The Dungeon' to your right.**

'Dungeon' is an old local word meaning a wooded valley. There is another steep-sided valley called 'The Dungeon' in Walk 15 at Thurstaston.

The bridge at Croughton, designed by Thomas Telford

5. At the end of field, cross another stile and go left from a footbridge. Do not go through the metal gate but walk up the long field keeping the hedge on your left. Eventually cross another stile and, at the far end of this field, turn left for 30 metres, then go right and continue ahead to a road, Little Rake Lane (as you go along this stretch you may be able to glimpse a private fishery behind a brick building to your right).

6. At the road junction, continue more or less straight ahead, along a road.

7. Bend left with the road. After 75 metres cross a stile tucked into the hedge on the right. Cross slightly right to the corner of the hedge ahead, then continue with the hedge on your left.

Once when I walked this route these fields were sour-smelling and an unnatural grey colour. They had recently been spread with pulped newspaper, which I have noticed on many other local fields. The pulp enriches the soil and is meant to be ploughed in soon after spreading.

8. **After about 300 metres, look for a stile and footbridge tucked into the hedge on your left (it's easy to miss). Cross, and walk ahead aiming for a stile by a large tree to the left of farm buildings. After the stile, continue straight ahead to another stile set in wooden fencing (you may have to negotiate some temporary fences). From here it's straight ahead to the final stile, by a tree at a road. Go left, back to the start.**

Walk 23: The 'Lost Settlement' of Hadlow

A mysterious 'lost settlement' – Roman, medieval and turnpike roads – a restored railway station – farmland – unusual trees

Start and finish	Hadlow Road Station car park ¼ mile (400 metres) south of the centre of Willaston. Willaston is signposted off the A540
Distance	4½ or 5¾ miles
Approximate time	Allow 2½ or 3 hours
Refreshments	Pubs and café in nearby Willaston; vending machines for drinks, sweets, etc. at Foxes Farm
Walking conditions	Flat; mostly good paths and tracks. Occasional muddy sections

This walk, mostly through quiet farming country, takes us across an area of mystery. It also gives a taste of several types of road and track spanning 2000 years of history, and visits a railway station restored to its 1950s look.

The railway was opened in 1866, linking Hooton (with its connections to Chester and Birkenhead) and Parkgate. The station was given the name 'Hadlow Road' to avoid confusion with another station at Willaston near Nantwich. The platform area, signal box, booking office and waiting room have all been restored to how they looked in 1952, four years before the last passenger train drew up here (the line remained open for freight traffic until 1962). There is also a short section of track, though the station actually had two platforms and two tracks, which merged into one at each end of the station.

1. **After looking around the station turn left at the main road and walk up Hadlow Road for just over 200 metres, then go left down New Hey Lane. After 200 metres go over a footbridge and stile to the right and continue ahead. Reach another stile, and continue in the same direction.**

Hadlow Road Station

A place called Edelaue is mentioned in the Domesday Book of 1086, compiled by the Norman conquerors. The fields where you are walking – the highest point in the area at 54 metres above sea level – have the peculiar name of 'Adler', pronounced similarly to Edelaue (try it with a French accent!). This, and other evidence, has led some local historians to suggest that there may once have been a settlement here, which was deserted hundreds of years ago – no one knows why. Any remains have now vanished but the local name 'Hadlow' comes from the Adler/Edelaue names. It has also been suggested that this location may have once been the meeting place of the leaders of the administrative area which once comprised the Wirral known as the 'hundred of Wilaveston'.

2. **Cross the driveway and go straight ahead, through trees with rhododendron bushes and a wall to your right. Cross a stile and continue to another.**

3. Cross the horse track and continue ahead, across the field, to reach a stile (broken at the time of writing) and gateway. Go left after these, following the field boundary to reach a footbridge and another stile at the field corner. Cross, and turn right; follow the field boundary, past a pond (actually old marl pits – see page 168), to reach the A540.

Have you noticed how there are often trees, generally oaks, spaced along the hedgerows? This is typical not just of the Willaston area, but elsewhere on the Wirral too. Throughout most of the 19th century, there was a huge demand for oak bark, which was used in Wirral's many leather tanneries. The trees were planted to meet

The ponds and tree lined hedges around Hadlow are typical of the Wirral landscape

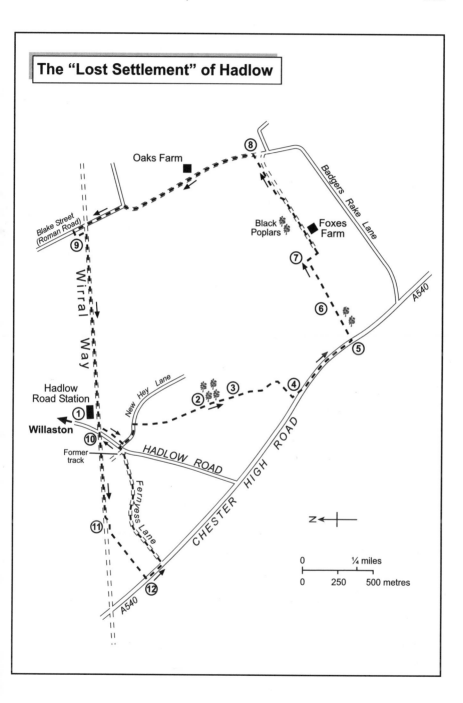

The "Lost Settlement" of Hadlow

this need and were meant to be felled. But demand suddenly dropped when mineral salts became used for tanning instead, and the trees were just left to grow.

4. **Turn left for 500 metres to reach and go through a metal kissing gate to the left (just before the road to Burton on the opposite side of the road).**

The line of the A540 has existed since medieval times, maybe longer. In 1787, it became a turnpike. These were roads operated by business trusts that built and maintained them in exchange for tolls charged to users. Previously the cost of maintaining roads had to be met by the local community but transferring the costs to road-users, via the trusts, meant rapid growth in the quantity and quality of roads. The improved network was a great force for economic expansion across Britain. A tollhouse was situated on the corner of Badgers Rake Lane, 500 metres beyond point 5.

Someone once asked me about the brick block on the pavement a few metres beyond the gate: it is a mounting block, used for getting on and off horses for riders leading their animals over the road.

5. **A few metres after the gate cross a stile (broken at the time of writing) and then continue ahead, with the hedge on your right, passing a few Austrian pines on the other side of the ditch. Reach and cross another stile.**

6. **Continue in the same direction with a hedge on your right, and then go straight across a very long field. The path may be indistinct but aim for a wooden post sticking up on the far side (in the past I've found that the farmer has grown his crops across the path; you are within your rights to walk through these crops provided you stick to the line of the path).**

7. **At the far side of the field turn right and soon turn left, keeping the hedge on your left, towards the buildings of Foxes Farm.**

The farm has popular riding stables. Vending machines with light refreshments are available here.

At the farm, continue ahead along a metalled track.

Almost immediately you pass three bungalows to your right. Look left here, about 150 metres across the field to a copse of trees behind a wooden fence. This is a designated Site of Special Scientific Interest as it contains black poplar trees, probably Britain's most endangered native tree. This site is particularly special as there is a pair of male and female trees here, one of very few such sites in the country. The seeds are regularly collected to help grow new trees elsewhere. Black poplars like wet conditions and these ones live in a marl pit.

Continue along the metalled track (ignore a sign that says 'Private Drive No admittance' just after the bungalows – you are on a public right of way). Some walkers choose to stay on this track to reach point 8 but, strictly, you should take the signed path through fields that starts 100 metres after the large farm buildings on your left, and runs parallel to the track – but be aware that this can be extremely muddy.

8. **At the T-junction with a farm road, turn left along it (again, don't be put off by the 'Private Road' sign). After about 1km (0.6 miles), when it reaches a minor road, bear left to follow this road, soon going over a hump-backed bridge.**

The line of the road ahead is believed to be part of a Roman Road called Blake Street that went from the North Gate of Roman Chester up the Wirral. It can be traced through most of the Willaston area and at some points before and afterwards. There were archaeological excavations along it in the 1960s.

9. **Immediately after the bridge, take the path left, doubling back on yourself. When you reach the Wirral Way turn right to follow the main path.**

The Way, Britain's first Country Park, was opened in 1973 following the path of the by-then disused railway from Hooton to West Kirby (the line had been extended there from Parkgate in 1886).

10. **For the shorter walk stop at the station. Otherwise, cross Hadlow Road and continue along the Wirral Way.**

11. Just after a large pylon to your right, go down steps to your left and through a kissing gate. Follow the right-hand field boundary until a few metres before a telegraph pole, where you should fork left along a rough path through the field, along a strip of very slightly higher ground towards a cream-coloured house at the far boundary of the field. Cross a stile, and continue to the A540.

12. Go left for 200m and then left again through a metal gate by a large oak tree, up a clear track. Continue to Hadlow Road. Cross it carefully and go left, back to the start.

This extra loop is included for you to enjoy the 'green lane' (an old grassy track) of Fernyess Lane. It is certainly 250 years old, and was very probably a medieval route to Ness (the name means it was the 'fern-covered lane to Ness'). From the Chester High Road, it led to a crossroads, where Hadlow Road, New Hey Lane, Fernyess Lane and another track, now vanished (see map), once met. Perhaps it was a major junction to access the mysterious Edelaue?

Walk 24. Little Neston and Ness

**Wirral's only coal mine – disused railway lines –
a deep railway cutting – ancient lanes – woodland –
saltmarsh – the Wirral Way**

Start and finish	Car park at end of Station Road, Neston. From the A540 Hinderton Arms, descend into Neston and turn left at the traffic lights; soon go left again at a mini-roundabout
Distance	4½ miles Can be cut short to 2¾ miles
Approximate time	Allow 2½ hours or 1½ for shorter route
Refreshments	The Wheatsheaf, Ness and The Harp, after point 7. Good picnic spot at Denhall Quay (between points 7 and 8) or near point 9
Walking conditions	Mostly easy walking over paths and tracks. A short section near point 3 can often be wet and muddy in winter

This is probably my favourite local route. The diversity of landscapes is extraordinary, from ancient tracks to remnants of the industrial revolution; and from a woodland haven to the grand expanse of the Dee saltmarsh. Each time you walk it, you will find something different to see. Before you start you may like to take a moment to look at the information board on the other side of the wooden fence by the car park

1. **From the car park walk under the railway bridge and up a residential road.**

This is Station Road and, through it is hard to believe now, the Hooton – West Kirby railway line once ran along here; there was a station towards the top end of the road on the right.

2. **At the top of the road cross straight over, through a wooden gate and down the slope.**

You are entering the amazing 800m cutting built for the railway in 1866, now part of the Wirral Way. On either side rises sandstone, the intersecting sloping layers of which were laid down by water flowing through a desert over 200 million years ago. Everywhere you can see shallow cuts in the rock, made by the picks of the 19th century navvies who carved out the cutting. The gradient is 1 in 72, considered steep for the steam trains at the time of building. They often struggled to climb the hill or to control their descent.

At the first of two bridges, both stained by locomotive soot, look for roman numerals carved into the stones each side of the arch. These helped the builders position them in the correct sequence. The cutting is dark and wet, suitable for only a few types of plant including ferns, ivy, mosses and liverworts. For more on the Wirral Way, see pages 50-51.

Soon after the path levels out, you pass large ponds to your left, tucked among trees and bushes. These are examples of marl pits, dug by local farmers since medieval times for their fertile sub-soil which was spread over nearby fields. Water has filled most old marl pits, turning them into ponds. You will find similar ponds all over the Wirral.

You then reach a section of railway embankment passing through beech and sycamore woodland. This is a lovely area at any time of year and always seems to be full of birdsong.

3. **Shortly before a narrow wooden bridge, go right down some concrete steps, over a stile, and turn right onto a track, Cuckoo Lane (in winter this section can sometimes be very muddy – you may find slightly drier ground at the edges of the track). 125 metres later, at a metal gate, continue up the hedged track.**

Cuckoo Lane oozes antiquity. It is part of a local network of ancient tracks used for cattle droving and packhorse transport. Centuries of use have turned the route into a 'holloway' – a sunken track, up

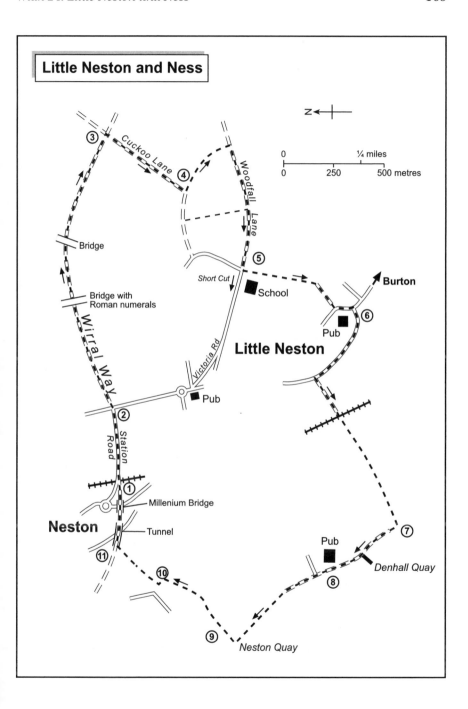

Little Neston and Ness

to 2 metres deep in places. Notice how it dries out as you climb from clay underfoot to sandstone.

4. **At the top of the hill, turn left through a metal kissing gate. Follow the field boundary to a stile and continue down the narrow path. At the track (Woodfall Lane), turn right.**

Most path boundaries around here are built with high banks reinforced by sandstone blocks. In past centuries these ensured that livestock driven up and down the old lanes did not stray into the adjacent fields, damaging crops – big fines could be levied if they did.

5. **At the tarmac road look for a path to the left, before the school. (If you want the shorter route continue down Woodfall Lane, and after 300 metres, fork right down Victoria Road. You reach a pub – the Royal Oak. Facing the pub, turn right, and soon go past a**

The remains of Denhall Quay, built in 1791 to take coal from Ness Colliery

mini-roundabout. **Continue to point 2 and retrace your steps to the start). For the full route, follow the path before the school to a stile and cross the field using the clear path bending slightly right. At the far corner, go down sandstone steps by terraced cottages into Cumbers Lane and continue ahead to the main road.**

Cumbers Lane is named after 'encumbrances' or obstructions once found in the fields here. These obstructions were probably boulders deposited here by melting glaciers after the last ice age.

Turn left to pass (or visit!) the pub.

You are now in the village of Ness, the birthplace of Emma Hamilton, Admiral Lord Nelson's mistress, who went from a life of poverty to being the foremost female 'celebrity' of her time. As the pavement bends right you pass Swan Cottage on the left, one of the places in the village that is claimed to be her birthplace.

6. **Immediately after the pub, go right, down Well Lane.**

Notice a granite boulder (an 'encumbrance' like those Cumbers Lane was named after) on the small triangular green at the road junction.

Continue for 300m to a track on the left with a small footpath sign, opposite 'New Heys'. Continue downhill for 800m, ignoring the paths into the housing estate; towards the bottom of the hill you fork left, off the tarmac path.

As you descend look ahead to the first line of hills in Wales. On the rounded brown hilltop sits Moel y Gaer, an Iron Age hillfort featured in Walk 26.

7. **Eventually reach a path T-junction. Turn right and soon join a track. After about 150 metres you come to the remains of Denhall Quay, jutting left.**

The sandstone quay was built in 1791 to serve Ness Colliery (an earlier quay, about 450 metres further along our route, has now disappeared). The colliery, and others with various names, operated on the land around you from 1759 to 1927 when local mining had become uneconomic. The coal seams were worked for well over a mile under the Dee and, in the early days, barges transported the coal along underground canals. They were propelled by 'legging' – people lay on their backs and pushed against the low roof of the tunnel.

Ness Colliery was very significant locally, being the first place on Wirral and west Cheshire to have a steam engine. Today we take engines and motors for granted, but it must have been extraordinary for people in the 1760s to witness for the first time a great machine heaving away and belching out black smoke through a tall chimney. Later, the great industrial engineer George Stephenson sent men to work on the engines here and almost certainly visited the mine himself. Some of the coal produced here would have been used to power the steam trains that chugged up and down the line along the Wirral Way, making the soot you saw earlier.

Continue, to reach The Harp Inn.

Various industries sprung up by Ness Colliery – brick, coke and charcoal making, metal ore smelting, and quicklime production for building and agriculture. The limestone was brought to Denhall Quay from North Wales and the remains of the kilns for heating it are just visible as grassy mounds in a garden behind the pub. Children as young as nine worked the mine and the labourers lived in appalling housing. In 1847 Ness village was described as 'the most miserable … mass of hovels' on the Wirral. The pub's walls are lined with pictures from the mine's later days.

8. **Continue in the same direction, past a metal gate, keeping parallel to the marsh.**

The ground around here consists largely of spoil from industrial activity. But to your left lies the great openness of the salt marsh. If you could cross to the river you'd notice a succession of plant types each adapted to the increasingly salty conditions found as the estuary's waters get closer. Here though, you soon pass huge stands of freshwater-loving common reed (the type used in

The colliery at Neston in the 1920s

thatching roofs) rustling in the wind. Today the marsh has a wild beauty, but the estuary has been unforgiving. Many people drowned before the marsh was formed as they misjudged the shifting sands while trying to cross to Chester or North Wales.

When the track ends continue along a clear marsh-side path. Eventually you reach a well-worn stone stile.

This is the site of Neston Key (also called the New Key and the Old Quay!), the site of another anchorage overtaken in importance by the port at Parkgate, and eventually stranded. It is extraordinary to think that, during the seventeenth century, this quiet spot buzzed with tens of thousands of passengers, as well as freight activity, going to or from Ireland and mainland Europe. During the English Civil War, in 1643, two thousand troops boarded ships here on a single day, bound for Ireland. As you cross the stile, the trees to your immediate right hide the remains of a brick building – The Key House – that once served the port. (The sandstone wall about 150m further along the coast, after a bridge, is a nice spot to detour to for a picnic).

9. **Take the gravel track that leads away from the marsh, eventually going through two kissing gates and over a wooden footbridge. At the top of the next field you go left a few metres, then go right through a kissing gate which is immediately after a wooden fence and a metal gate.**

10. **Take the path ahead past a telegraph pole.**

The line of hedges to left and right by the telegraph pole marks the disused railway branch line to the colliery area.

Go straight ahead, up the field, to reach a kissing gate.

11. **To return to the car park turn right along the Wirral Way, passing over the attractive Millennium Bridge, with its railway decoration and poetry.**

Neston Colliery in about 1875, from a painting by Arthur Suker

You may first like to look at an unusual little tunnel which the Way passes over. For this, cross straight over the Way from the field path and then go right a few metres down the road. It is said that when circuses used to come to Neston, elephants would go down on their knees to crawl through this tunnel. After this detour retrace your steps to the Wirral Way and go left back to the car park.

Walk 25: Puddington and Shotwick

A menagerie – ancient and pretty villages – a large pigeon house – redwood trees – masons' marks

Start and finish	The Yacht at Two Mills on the A540
Distance	5¼ miles
Approximate time	Allow 2½ to 3 hours
Refreshments	The Yacht, a good spot for the walk to end
Walking conditions	Roads, tracks and field-paths (the latter can be muddy after rain between points 3 and 5)

These are two of Wirral's most ancient and attractive villages, both recorded in the Domesday Book of 1086. Puddington has two large Halls. The older one was owned by the Massey family, who were surrounded by tales of intrigue and derring-do for 500 years. Shotwick, with its ancient church, was once a main crossing point into Wales and also an important port. The site of its castle is featured in Walk 17.

This Walk has a little more road-walking than usual, but the lanes are quiet and the surrounding country attractive.

The Yacht's origins go back for hundreds of years. In 1722 it was The Ship but later that century became The Yacht, named after the Royal Yacht that sailed between Parkgate and Dublin – the pub is exactly halfway between Chester and Parkgate and was much used by travellers between the two places.

1. **Cross the A540 and turn left. Pass the grounds of a boarding kennels with its permanent private menagerie including alpacas, ostriches, rheas, pygmy and angora goats, and a Vietnamese pot-bellied pig called Felicity!**

The A540 is an old turnpike road. See page 164 for more details.

2. **250 metres before the traffic lights, by the large road sign, cross the dual carriageway and go down Walden Drive. Go through a gate, and straight ahead over two stiles. In the works yard, keep to the left, right next to the hedge and behind a container and portacabin, to reach another stile at the A550.**

3. **Cross with care, go left 15 metres, then through a kissing gate and over a stile. Go straight ahead, keeping the fence on your left, to cross a stream.**

This is Shotwick Brook, which rises in Neston and once flowed into the Dee at Shotwick. West-flowing streams are rare on the Wirral. Almost all the other streams and rivers eventually flow into the Mersey.

4. **Turn right, and walk for the next 650 metres keeping the field boundary (variously a ditch, hedge or fence) to your immediate right all the time; you cross a stile at one point along the way. You bend left after the house and eventually cross a footbridge and stile to reach the road.**

Shortly before the final stile you pass some ponds in the trees to your right. These are marl pits – now flooded with rain water – dug in past centuries as a source of nutrients to spread on the land to increase fertility. There are numerous pits like this across the Wirral.

Note the unusual thatched house opposite the stile, with thatched foxes on the roof!

You never know what you will stumble across at the menagerie!

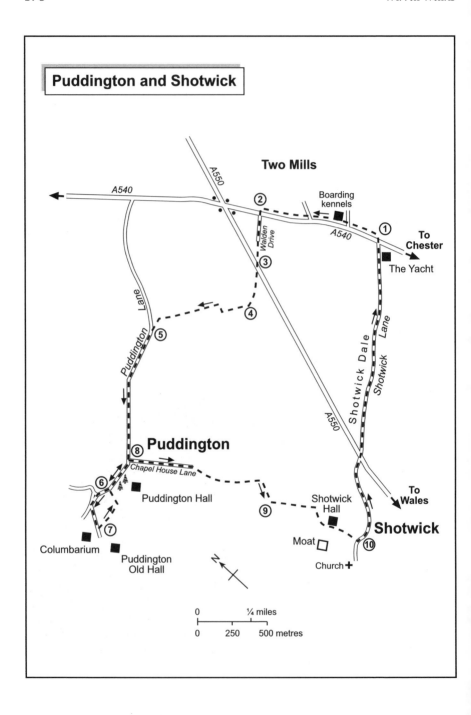

Puddington and Shotwick

Two Mills

A540

A550

Walden Drive

Boarding kennels

① To Chester

The Yacht

②

③

④

⑤

Puddington Lane

Shotwick Dale

Shotwick Lane

A550

Puddington

⑧ Chapel House Lane

Puddington Hall

⑥

⑦

Columbarium

Puddington Old Hall

⑨

Shotwick Hall

Moat

Church

⑩ Shotwick

To Wales

N

0   ¼ miles
0   250   500 metres

5. **Turn left and continue to Puddington along the road.**

Just after Chapel House Lane glimpse Puddington Hall on the left through the trees. (This is the latest of three Halls that Puddington has had. You'll see the earliest one in a little while; the third one burnt down in the 1860s, on a site just off our route). There are two magnificent Giant Sequoia trees (also called *Wellingtonia* after the Duke of Wellington) at the entrance to a driveway, next to the Hall's converted stable block. A useful fact for a trivia quiz is that this bark is fire resistant!

6. **In the centre of Puddington, keep left of the telephone box, and follow the road round left down Old Hall Lane, which has several attractive old buildings.**

After 100m, stop by the telegraph pole on your left.

Converted farm buildings in Puddington

The long building ahead of you, slightly left, is Puddington Old Hall, the oldest part dating from 1490, (although it does not look particularly old from this angle). It was built around a courtyard and once had a moat. In the Middle Ages, moats were not necessarily a means of defence, but were common status symbols amongst the better off. The Hall was owned by the Massey family for 700 years. One famous tale relates to William Massey who left the Battle of Preston in 1715. He rode the 46 miles home hell for leather, crossing the Mersey where it could be forded in those days, between Speke and Hooton. When he arrived at Puddington his exhausted horse is said to have dropped dead on the flagstones.

Wander a few metres up the 'Private Drive' to your right (it's OK - it's a public footpath). Here you will find a squarish brick 'columbarium', or pigeon house - one of only two on the Wirral. Pigeons and doves were popular winter food until about 1800, and pigeon houses (also called dovecotes) became a common feature of larger farms, particularly when the farms were owned by the lord of the manor such as the Masseys. They fell out of favour when the development of winter root crops meant that animals could be kept and fed over the winter - previously most were killed in the autumn and their meat was dried and salted. As well as

The columbarium (pigeon house) at Puddington

being a food source, pigeons also supplied dung - called 'guano' - which was a valuable fertiliser (and an ingredient for gunpowder!). This columbarium is odd in having corners that are not quite square.

7. **Take the path left after the telegraph pole. This leads you back to Puddington Lane - turn right, retracing your earlier steps for 250 metres.**

8. **Go along Chapel House Lane (named after a Catholic chapel belonging to one of the earlier Halls). Stay on the road, which eventually forks right through a wide gateway, following a footpath sign. 100 metres later go left alongside a hedge. At the hedge-end, go half-right across the field to pass right of a pond. Continue to the field edge and turn right.**

To your left are a ditch and a bank topped by a hedge. These may well be of medieval origin, marking the ancient boundaries between Burton and Shotwick parishes.

9. **At the bottom corner of the field turn left through a double gate. Keep the fence to your right, through a gate to join a green lane, hedged on each side, and then a track. Follow this as it bends right, and go on into the village of Shotwick.**

On your left you pass the picturesque E-shaped Shotwick Hall, built in 1662. This replaced an earlier Hall situated amongst the clump of trees 125 metres to your right. The building has disappeared but its moat survives, surrounding the trees.

Take time to explore picturesque Shotwick. Most of the houses have great character, and the church has many fascinating features. Look for Greyhound Farm: if you are looking down the road towards the church it is just after the Victorian post-box in the wall on your left. This was once the Greyhound Inn and became notorious as the place where runaway lovers were married illegally by the local curate – a kind of English Gretna Green.

Shotwick church is fascinating and there is not space here to cover everything. There is some excellent information dotted around inside the church – here are a few other unusual things to notice. There has been a stone church here since Norman times. The wall each side of the porch, made of uneven sandstone blocks, is almost 1000 years old, as is the carved stone archway above the main door. The inside of the porch itself has several vertical grooves. These are said to date from the 1300s when Edward III banned football and made everyone practice archery on a Sunday after mass instead. The grooves are said to be where the archers sharpened their arrows.

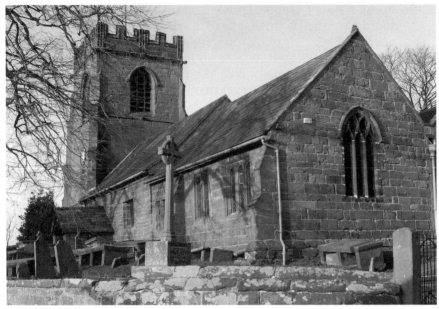

Shotwick Church

Stonemasons used to leave individual distinguishing marks on the stones they cut. If you enter the tower, you can see one immediately on your right, at about eye level. Several others are visible elsewhere on the tower walls (see illustration). This tower was built in about 1500, around the same time and to the same plan as the towers at Backford (Walk 22), Handley and Tattenhall (all in West Cheshire). Several of the same mason's marks can be seen at all four churches, showing that the workmen travelled to where the work was.

10. **After exploring the village go up the road (which starts off as a sunken lane, below the level of the adjacent fields, due to centuries of heavy use). Cross Shotwick Brook (again), and then, very carefully, the A550. Continue uphill along Shotwick Lane, through pretty Shotwick Dale, back to the start.**

A mason's mark on the wall of the tower in Shotwick Church

Walk 26: Halkyn Mountain Common

A different perspective on Wirral – old mining landscape – an Iron Age hillfort – fantastic views – quarrying – lime kilns

Start and finish	Gravelled area on the bend just above the church in the centre of Rhosesmor village. For Rhosesmor take the signed turn off the northbound A55 just after the Little Chef on your left. Go left at the Britannia Inn and then left at a T-junction onto the B5123. Continue for about 1¾ miles
Distance	6½ miles (for a shorter version, explore all or part of the high ground between points 1 and 8)
Approximate time	Allow 3 to 4 hours
Refreshments	None directly on the route but there are pubs at Rhosesmor (Red Lion), Rhes-y-cae (Miners' arms) and Halkyn (Britannia Inn and Blue Bell Inn). Point 8 is a good picnic spot
Walking conditions	Mostly grassy paths and firm tracks. Occasional road. One short climb at the start

'Compare and contrast' they used to tell us at school, and this route certainly gives you a completely different perspective on Wirral, starting across the Dee in the first line of hills in Wales. Not only are there magnificent views across to Wirral, and beyond (take binoculars if you have them), but you also get a fascinating and diverse landscape in its own right with many points of contrast to our own.

The route is criss-crossed by other paths or tracks, so don't worry if you lose the suggested route occasionally – just take a logical route between the main landmarks.

1. **From the parking spot, walk up the steep tarmac track which, by Rock Cottage, becomes a grassy path adjacent to a quarry.**

   There are fossils in the fence-pillars of the quarry, which is small compared to the vast, still-worked ones you will probably spot later (incidentally, if you hear a siren sound, they are about to blast some rock in one of the big quarries). The underlying rock throughout this walk is limestone – older and harder than the sandstone that Wirral is made from. The same limestone also forms the Great Orme at Llandudno, and Eglwyseg Mountain above Llangollen. Limestone is used as building stone, and also yields lime, used in agriculture and as an ingredient to make mortar. The lime used to be extracted from the rock using large kilns like the one you will see near the end of this walk.

2. **Follow the path round to the top of the quarry; turn right by a slightly pointed stone fence pillar, along a path between gorse. After 40m, you reach rising ground to right and left – the ramparts of Moel y Gaer, an Iron Age hillfort.**

A circuit of Moel y Gaer gives breathtaking views

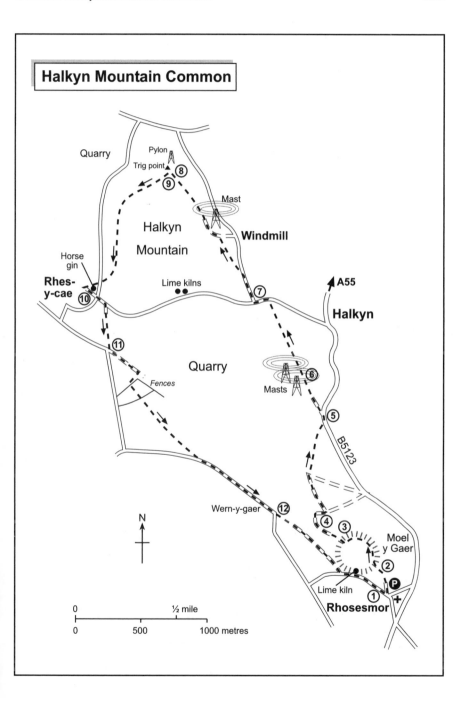

Halkyn Mountain Common

The ramparts comprise a circular bank and an outer ditch, some 180m in diameter. With commanding views in every direction (it is worth walking a full circuit of the perimeter), this amazing feat of construction would have provided an excellent defence for its inhabitants some 2000-2500 years ago. A defendable site was needed because of increased competition for land. Archaeological excavation has shown that the hilltop was in use even earlier – in Neolithic time about 5500 years ago.

This is the highest point along these hills, some 303 metres/950 feet above sea level. The Clwydian Hills stretch off to the south-west, including Moel Famau with a 'blip' on top (actually the Jubilee Tower); and you can see the Pennines in the far distance to the east. (The raised, square area in the centre of the hillfort is just a covered reservoir).

At Burton Point on Wirral there is also a defensive enclosure, thought to be Iron Age like Moel y Gaer's. However, it is only small, and its history is far less well understood than that of Moel y Gaer.

3. **On the north-west side of the hillfort, find a narrow path that runs downhill past an electricity pole about 30 metres from the ramparts, and then past a small fenced off area. Descend and cross to a light-coloured track to the left of a house and outbuilding.**

As you descend you notice the extraordinary pockmarked landscape. This is mining country and, since Roman times (maybe earlier), people have worked to extract lead and zinc that has formed in the fissures of the rock. Throughout this walk, you will pass hollows and mounds, the latter formed as people dumped spoil from their mining activity. The plots on which houses sit tend to be scattered across the landscape rather than concentrated in a single area, probably established by miners years ago working on their chosen site. The last mine closed in 1986.

4. **Follow the track and it soon doubles back on itself and then meets a road. Turn left along the road and continue to some houses, called River View, at the apex of a sharp right-hand bend. At this apex continue ahead along a broad green path.**

5. At the B5123, go left a few metres, then up the track to the right of the black and white chevron sign.

6. Walk between the two masts and the houses and continue ahead, passing a garden on your right with hedge-trees around its boundary. Sometimes you will be on a path, sometimes a track – your general direction is towards a single mast to the north-north-west.

7. At a road, take the signed route to 'Windmill'. Just before you reach the bungalow on the left, fork left off the road and walk alongside the bungalow's fence, still in the general direction of the mast. When you reach a track go left and follow it past the mast. Continue, and on the sharp right-hand bend, 10m after the gate of Roseberry Villa, turn left to find a narrow path, heading roughly towards the highest pylon you can hopefully see in the distance. Later the path widens, passing between gorse bushes, and you continue in the general direction of the pylon.

A miner's bell pit on the Common

8. **75m before the pylon, and just before a trig point (the pyramidal concrete pillar) on a mound off to your left, turn left down a clear path. In a moment you will continue down this path but first, however, clamber up to the trig point to take in the excellent views.**

You can pick out details of the Wirral, with the shining white houses of Parkgate particularly standing out. The less easily eroded limestone means that on this ridge you are always some 500 ft (160m) higher than any part of sandstone Wirral. Further away, Liverpool's cathedrals are clearly visible. Up the coast, you can make out Formby Point and, possibly, Blackpool Tower. On a clear day, you can even make out the mountains of the Lake District some 75 miles away.

Trig points ('trig' being short for 'trigonometrical'; they are also known as triangulation pillars) were made as part of a process started in the 1930s to map the whole of the UK accurately. 6,173 were built and the job was not finished until 1962. My guess is that the most visited trig point on the Wirral is on Thurstaston Hill (Walk 11).

With your back to the Wirral, look half right, down the hill, about 75 metres away. There are several excellent examples of 'bell-pits' – circular mounds made from the spoil being thrown out from a central mine shaft.

9. **Continue on the path mentioned previously and go downhill (passing more bell-pits of various sizes). Ignore crossing paths but fork left where the path splits just after a large horizontal slab of limestone to your right. You are aiming for the houses just visible to your half-left.**

The slabs are caps to old mine shafts; you can also find many beehive shaped stone cairns capping the mines around here.

When the ground becomes flatter go straight over at cross-paths near bracken, soon afterwards bearing right to eventually meet the road opposite a playground at Rhes-y-cae. Cross the road and continue with the playground to your left.

Just overlapping the far right-hand corner of the schoolyard you will find a 12m diameter grassy circular ditch. This was once the site of a horse gin – a winding mechanism for the mines, powered by a horse walking round in circles (making the ditch) turning a wide drum, mounted on a large central pole, with a rope wrapped around it.

10. **Go left along a track and, at a road junction, cross to take the road signposted 'Halkyn', heading slightly uphill. 150 metres after the junction turn right down a track between cottages (the left-hand one is called Fron Oleu). After the house on the left, as the track bends right, go ahead down a grassy path.**

Crossing the Common in snow

11. **At the bottom of the hill, before the road, go left up a track. After about 250 metres, near a field corner to your right, turn right and follow the wire fence to find a stile tucked in the fence. Cross it, and keep in the same direction to another stile. Continue in the same direction up a long grassy field, soon running parallel to another fence to cross two further stiles. After the last one continue in the same direction, eventually joining the road. Stay on this for 750m/½ mile, into Wern-y-gaer.**

12. **At a bend, by the black and white chevron sign, go straight ahead, along a narrow grassy path, parallel to a single line of cable to your left. Ignore paths to right and left; eventually you reach a track to the left of a cream bungalow; go along this to meet a road. Turn left back to the start.**

The large lime kiln by Moel y Gaer

Along the final stretch of road, you pass a lime kiln on your left. Rock was loaded through the hole on top of the kiln and burnt at 900 degrees centigrade or more. This produced quicklime which was then used in building and agriculture. Lime is an agricultural fertiliser and the kilns were a big factor in helping feed a rapidly growing population in the early 1800s.

Limekilns were also built on the Wirral - there were many dotted along the Dee shore, for example – though they were probably smaller than this one. Boulders of limestone would have been transported across the Dee from Wales in boats for processing. (The alternative of transporting ready-made quicklime was asking for trouble: it is highly corrosive and, mixed with any water in the bowels of a boat, would have quickly corroded and sunk it!)

Walk 27: A Wirral Shore-to-Shore Trail: Parkgate to Eastham

A fine route, right across the Wirral

Start	The 'Donkey Stand' on The Parade at Parkgate (jutting into the marsh about 25 metres north of Nicholls ice cream shop)
Finish	Eastham Country Park Visitor Centre
Transport	If possible, leave a car at the end or arrange to be met. Alternatively, plan around public transport routes that cross the trail – buses visit both ends and points in between. **Note:** much of the route is suitable for cycles – use local maps to join the road and track sections together
Distance	10½ miles for the full walk. Otherwise, split the route into two or three sections for a series of outings
Refreshments	Pubs and cafés at the start, finish and at Willaston (3½ miles); Dibbinsdale pub after 6½ miles
Walking conditions	Generally very good paths and firm tracks. The short track at point 5 and the field at 7 can be muddy after rain. There is a short section of tunnel at point 12: you may like a torch but it is not essential. At point 8 you have a choice of routes which enables you to avoid a narrow stretch of road without a pavement if you prefer

*Here's a fine challenge, to walk (or cycle) Wirral from shore to shore –
from the Dee at Parkgate to the Mersey at Eastham. Along the way, we
take in some of Wirral's finest countryside and beauty spots, including
three Country Parks. With good paths and only the occasional gentle
uphill, the walk is within most people's capabilities. It would make a
fine outing for country-lovers, families wanting a challenge or
sponsored walkers seeking a novel route.*

*Some of this route uses other routes mentioned in this book so,
rather than duplicating information, I've given page numbers where
you can find more information about what you can see along the way.*

1. **Walk south from the Donkey Stand and turn left up Station Road
   for 250 metres. Turn right at the 'Wirral Country Park' sign,
   going straight
   ahead at the top of
   the slope to join the
   Wirral Way for
   1.25km/¾ mile.**

Wirral Way information: pages 50-51. *Parkgate information (and an
old photo of the donkey stand): pages 101-2 and 107.*

2. **Shortly after the red metal Millennium Bridge, go straight ahead
   under the rail bridge and up a residential road. At the T-junction
   continue straight ahead, along the path for another 2.6km/1.6
   miles.**

Information on the amazing railway cutting: page 168.

   **You will go through a short concrete tunnel, under the A540.
   Immediately afterwards make sure you take the gate to the
   left.**

3. **Keep an eye open for a large pylon in a field to your right.
   Immediately before the pylon turn left down the marked path,
   alongside a wire fence. Pass a large pond (actually a marl pit,
   see page 168). (If you'd like to visit Willaston's quaint Hadlow
   Road Station restored to its 1950s look, stay on the Wirral Way
   for another 400 metres. Information on the station is on page
   160).**

The Wirral Way

The path bends right and later becomes a track, then a small residential road leading to the Pollard Inn car park. Walk down the brick drive to the right hand side of the pub building to emerge onto Willaston Green.

Willaston Green information: pages 117-8.

4. **Cross the main road, turn left for a few metres and turn right along the path just before the churchyard. When you reach a residential road, go half-left looking for a gap in the wall by the footpath sign. Take the path and, emerging at playing fields, keep to the right-hand boundary (or take a short detour around Willaston Meadow – see pages 118-9). Keep straight ahead for about 450 metres going through a gate and crossing stiles. Reach a road, and turn right.**

Mill information: page 119.

5. **After 150 metres turn left along a track, signposted to Raby. After another 150 metres turn right across stone steps and a stile. Walk gently downhill, with the field boundary to your left. Keep straight ahead for about 1km (0.6 miles), crossing stiles and footbridges.**

6. **Emerge at a road, Benty Heath Lane. Turn left and walk for 350 metres. As the road bends left turn right, along a lane with a footpath sign, past a pair of brick semi-detached houses.**

7. **Immediately after crossing the motorway turn left, over a stile, and walk along the field edge parallel to the motorway. At a stile cross and turn right to go along a grassy path and reach a golf course.**

The route here is not well signed, but cross the fairway more-or-less straight ahead, passing right of the nearest birch tree, to pick up a faint grass-trodden path. You will see a 'Public Footpath' sign on metal legs, and pass to the left of a stand of three tall, graceful conifers. Keep on roughly the same heading, passing another sign, to eventually reach a stile at the road. Turn right.

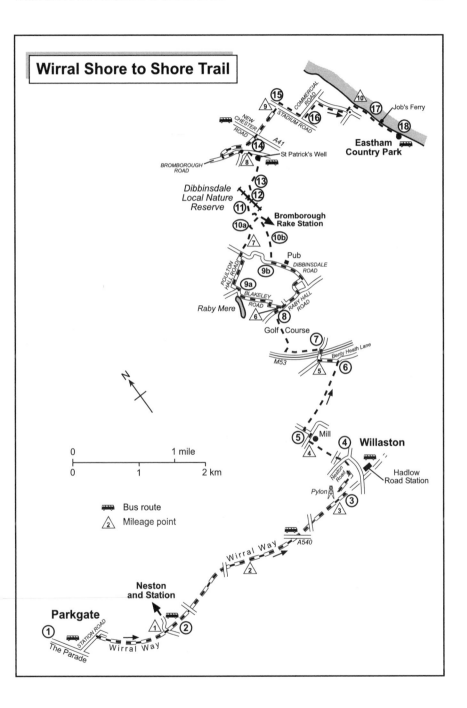

The octagonal public footpath sign at the road had recently been painted when I last visited – done as part of a local scheme involving young offenders to maintain the many such posts across the Wirral.

8. **You have a choice now. One option, (a), is to go via Raby Mere, a lovely spot, but requiring a walk of 700 metres/½ mile along a narrow, winding, uphill stretch of road without a pavement. The alternative, (b), almost entirely on good pavements, goes through a pleasant residential area (with a pub) before entering attractive woodland,**

   For (a) go 75 metres along Raby Hall Road, then go left along Blakeley Road, and walk to Raby Mere.

   The mere is an artificial lake, created as a pond to power a watermill in the early 17th century.

   For (b) continue along Raby Hall Road, down into the dip and up the other side of the valley. Take the first left, into Barrymore Way, staying on it when it later bends right. At a T-junction, Dibbinsdale Road, go left, passing the pub after 300 metres.

9. **Continuing with (a): Descend Poulton Hall Road, and continue, to climb out of the valley along the narrow road. At the T-junction look for a 'Public Footpath' sign across the large field, taking the path to pass a telegraph pole.**

   Continuing with (b): 250 metres after the pub, while descending the hill (there is a very short stretch without a pavement here), look for a metal kissing gate on the right to enter Marfords Wood.

   Marfords Wood is an ancient woodland (see point 10 below) and in spring is carpeted with wood anemones and then bluebells – plants which often indicate these old woods.

   The good path crosses a little stream via a footbridge; 50 metres later there is a fork in the path, each side of a tree. Go left here, gently downhill, and soon reach and cross a footbridge over the Dibbin.

The bridge over the Dibbin is called Ladybridge. There has been one on this site for over 700 years – one was built of timber from Marfords Wood in 1274.

There are pretty ponds here – look out for grey herons perched in the water or flying overhead. These ponds are man-made and the reeds in them act as a natural filter for polluted water which makes its way here after falling on the M53 motorway.

Wood anemones in spring: signs of an ancient woodland

10. **Continuing with (a): at the field corner, follow the main path. Take time to read the interpretation board near the top of Bodens Hey Meadow, then follow the path downhill, keeping to the right-hand side of the meadow with woodland to your right. Near the bottom of the hill, by another interpretation board, turn left along a main path along the bottom of the meadow.**

Continuing with (b): Continue along the clear path between the ponds. Soon after the ponds end, go right when the path forks to take the main path along the bottom of the meadow (stop at the fork, though, to read the interpretation board ahead of you).

(a) and (b) You are in Dibbinsdale Local Nature Reserve which has much natural interest, containing woodland, meadows, reed swamps, parkland and grassland. Dibbinsdale Wood, on the opposite side of the valley (you will cross into it shortly), is especially important as it is believed to be the largest area of 'ancient woodland' on Merseyside i.e. land that's been continually wooded since trees started growing after the last ice age. The dominant trees today are ash and oak, but there are also wych elm, sycamore, beech, and hornbeam. Dibbinsdale has been designated a Site of Special Scientific Interest.

11. **Cross two adjacent wooden bridges over the stream. 20 metres after the second, bend left along the main path.**

It is hard to imagine today but the river here was tidal until the 19th century when Spital Dam was built downstream. The dam prevented water from the Mersey at Bromborough Pool rising past this point and all the way to Poulton Bridge another 600 metres/⅓mile upstream.

Soon after taking the main path, just before a wooden bench on the right, you can find two hornbeams on the right, an uncommon tree this far north, with grey-green rippled bark. There are others nearby that came down in the great winds of January 2007. Amazingly, the fallen trees are continuing to grow.

12. **At a high railway embankment, ignore the steps up; go through a tunnel, named 'Otter Bridge'.**

The bridge was named by workmen, building the railway embankment in the late 1830s, who saw many otters playing here. Sadly, none has been seen since the 1863. Keep an eye open for kingfishers along the stream though.

13. **Keep to this path, passing stands of tall, graceful common reed. Go right at a path T-junction, keeping to the level ground.**

Cross another wooden bridge and, a few metres later, take the right-hand path uphill, with a fence on your right.

100 metres later, at a cross-paths, go straight ahead, initially downhill. Ignore the path left at the foot of the hill; instead climb to reach a bench at a good viewpoint over the river and beyond.

Reed beds thrive in the valley bottom; around them is 'carr woodland' – regularly flooded areas which suit willow, alder and dogwood.

From the viewpoint keep straight ahead, keeping to the edge of the hillside. 60 metres after the viewpoint, fork left along a lesser, non-gravelled, path still along the top edge of the hill, between trees. Continue ahead, gradually descending sandstone

cliffs, to reach a path at the bottom. Continue ahead and, when you soon meet other main paths, look out for St. Patrick's Well tucked into the hillside to your right.

The well is said to have been blessed by Saint Patrick in the fifth century AD and the waters are supposed to possess healing powers for the eyes.

Continue ahead to eventually meet a road.

14. **At the road turn left, and go straight ahead at the mini-roundabout, up Bromborough Road, passing a World War II pillbox. Notice the 13-metre-high embankment to your right, over the River Dibbin at Spital Dam (incidentally the name 'Spital' comes from a nearby lepers' 'ho-*spital*' in the Middle Ages). Walk uphill for 300m. At railings turn right through a gap in the wall and join the Cycleway/Footpath for 1km (0.6 miles), initially walking parallel to the stretch of road you've just walked up.**

The rest of the route, until you reach the boundary of Eastham Country Park, has, perhaps, a surprising significance. It follows, almost precisely, the line of railways constructed by Lever Brothers from 1910 to link their factories at Port Sunlight and Bromborough Port, and to give access to docks on the Mersey and to the main Birkenhead – Chester railway line. Numerous branch lines came off the route and even the right-hand turns that our walking route makes mirror the many turns made by the railways.

The route soon goes over the embankment you saw earlier. Before long you enter a railway cutting that is 9 metres deep, passing under the New Chester Road.

15. **At the white barrier take the zig-zag path uphill. Turn left at the top to go over the path you have just walked along. Go straight ahead along Stadium Road for 350 metres.**

This is not a beautiful area but you may wish to walk along the cycleway which has been very pleasantly landscaped and is, I've found, surprisingly full of birdsong.

16. Turn left down Commercial Road, following the Cycleway/ Footpath sign.

Take the next right, still following the cycleway. Just before the roundabout immediately after the massive Meyer Prestige building, turn left to walk towards the Mersey alongside green railings. Follow the obvious path to reach a small car park.

To your right once stood Bromborough Power Station. The railway ran along this stretch too, parallel to the river, stopping near the small car park at the end.

17. After the small car park, go straight ahead through a gap in the railings to stay parallel with the river. At a rise in the path, look for a gate in the railings to the left. Down the steps is Job's Ferry.

Job's Ferry information: page 60.

18. Continue and turn right at the mini-roundabout to reach the Eastham Country Park Visitor Centre.

Eastham Country Park information: page 59.

Congratulations!
You have walked Wirral from 'Shore to Shore'.

Also from Sigma Leisure:

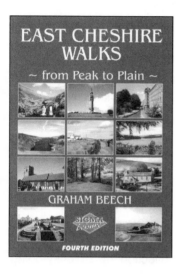

East Cheshire Walks
from Peak to Plain 4th Edition
Graham Beech
The definitive guide to walking in East Cheshire is now in its fourth edition! Completely updated and revised, with nearly 40 walks covering 250 miles, there really is something for everyone. Footpath diversions fully documented.
£8.99

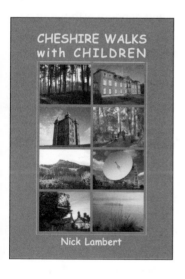

**Cheshire Walks With Children
2nd Edition**
Nick Lambert
Now completely revised and updated, this was the first in our "walks with children" series and has quickly become a firm favourite. There are 30 walks, ranging in length, together with things to look out for and questions to answer along the way make it an entertaining book for young and old alike.
£8.99

All-Terrain Pushchair Walks
Cheshire
Norman Buckley

30 graded walks, from level routes around pretty Cheshire villages to more adventurous hikes across the hillsides. Detailed directions and a map are provided for each route, together with some stunning photographs.

£7.95

Best Tea Shop Walks in the Peak District
Norman and June Buckley

A wonderful collection of 26 easy-going walks that are ideal for families and all those who appreciate fine scenery with a touch of decadence in the shape of an afternoon tea or morning coffee —or both!

£7.95

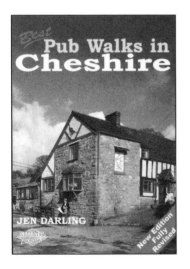

Best Pub Walks in Cheshire 2nd Edition
Jen Darling

This is the second edition of a guidebook to the walks and pubs of Cheshire.

"I was delighted to be asked to put a few words on paper ... this book brings together a series of suggestions for your enjoyment."
– John Ellis, Cheshire Tourism

£7.95

Discovering Manchester
2nd Edition
Barry Worthington

This stylish walking guide doubles as a detailed account of the city's architecture, its history and tourism attractions. There are walks throughout Manchester including such major entertainment and cultural centres as the Bridgewater Hall, Urbis, the Museum of Science and Industry, the Lowry and many more. Explore the entire city – from the Corn Exchange to G-Mex, from the Cathedral to Affleck's Palace.

9.99

Available July 2010

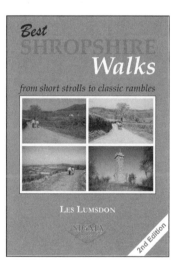

Best Shropshire Walks 2nd Edition
From short strolls to classic rambles
Les Lumsdon

A new revised edition of this much loved guide contains 36 walks, including 12 completely new routes, located in all parts of the county. Several walks feature fine hill walking on the Welsh borders and others start from delightful villages and hamlets in the north and east of the county.

£8.99

Archaeology Walks in The Peak District
Ali Cooper

These walks explore archaeological sites where there are visible pre-historic features in the landscape: Bronze age barrows, stone circles, caves, mines and much more. Walks are from 3 to 12 miles and are fully illustrated. The book includes an introduction to the study of archaeology and a glossary of the terminology used. Brief descriptions of the major finds on the walks are included, plus a bibliography for those who wish to delve deeper. Ali Cooper has an MA in archaeology and is a keen outdoors enthusiast.

£8.99

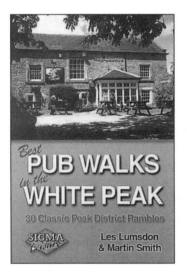

Best Pub Walks in the Dark Peak & Best Pub Walks in the White Peak
Les Lumsdon and Martin Smith

These two books, both by Les Lumsdon and Martin Smith, provide comprehensive coverage of the entire Peak District. Inspiring walks and welcoming pubs enable walkers to appreciate the history, landscape and personalities of the area. These books were published by us originally in the 1980s and have recently been completely updated to ensure accuracy. Each book costs *£8.99*

Derbyshire Walks with Children
William D Parke

All these walks are less than six miles long, with 'escape routes' for the young or less energetic. *"The needs, entertainment and safety of children have been of paramount importance."*
– Peak Advertiser
£8.99

Peak District Walking – On The Level
Norman Buckley

Some folk prefer easy walks, and sometimes there's just not time for an all-day yomp. In either case, this is definitely a book to keep on your bookshelf. Norman Buckley has had considerable success with "On The Level" books for the Lake District and the Yorkshire Dales.

The walks are ideal for family outings and the precise instructions ensure that there's little chance of losing your way. Well-produced maps encourage everybody to try out the walks - all of which are well scattered across the Peak District.
£7.95

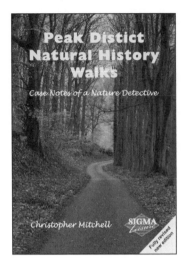

Peak District Walking Natural History Walks
Christopher Mitchell

An updated 2nd Edition with 18 varied walks for all lovers of the great outdoors — and armchair ramblers too! Learn how to be a nature detective, a 'case notes' approach shows you what clues to look for and how to solve them. Detailed maps include animal tracks and signs, landscape features and everything you need for the perfect natural history walk. There are mysteries and puzzles to solve to add more fun for family walks — solutions supplied! Includes follow on material with an extensive Bibliography and 'Taking it Further' sections.

£8.99

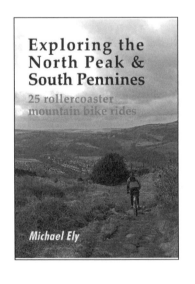

Exploring the North Peak & South Pennines
25 rollercoaster mountain bike rides
Michael Ely

This book will inspire you to pump up the tyres and oil the chain for some excitement, exercise and a feast of rollercoaster riding as you join Michael Ely on some great mountain biking in these Pennine hills. Over 500 miles of riding for the adventurous off-road cyclist that explore the tracks and steep lanes in the Pennine hills. There are twenty-five illustrated rides - with cafe stops half way round - to provide both a challenge and many hours of healthy exercise in classic mountain biking country.

£8.99

Available July 2010

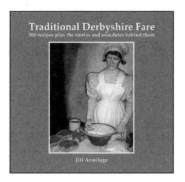

Traditional Derbyshire Fare
300 recipes plus the stories and anecdotes behind them
Jill Armitage

Some Derbyshire dishes are well known, like the Bakewell Pudding; many more, including some of the most delectable, are little known outside the places whose name they bear. The recipes are individual, easy, economical, with readily available ingredients, and have a strong regional accent. This is Derbyshire food at its best.
£12.95

Derbyshire Crime and Punishment
Over the centuries
Peter J Naylor

Crime fascinates us all, particularly murders, and the bloodier they are the better they are received. It would appear that the Peak District was a lawless place until more recent times. Whilst this book gives much of its space over to murder, other crimes are also included.
£8.99

Available July 2010

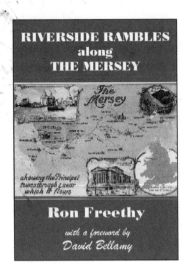

Riverside Rambles along The Mersey
Ron Freethy
with a foreword by David Bellamy

This is far more than a guidebook for walkers, it is also a portrait of one of the world's greatest rivers – once so polluted that Michael Heseltine described the state of the Mersey basin as "an affront to civilised society". Nowadays, however, salmon pass through the estuary, wildlife abounds along the entire catchment area and a rich and diverse coastline attracts a huge variety of birdlife.

Featuring 30 walks short, gentle walks (mostly circular). Explore the unique scenery, ecology and heritage of this area.
£8.99